The Role of
the Trustee

The Role of
the Trustee

ORLEY R. HERRON, JR.

Assistant to the President
Indiana State University

INTERNATIONAL TEXTBOOK COMPANY

Scranton, Pennsylvania

Printed in the United States of America by
The Haddon Craftsmen, Inc., Scranton, Pennsylvania.

Library of Congress Catalog Card Number: 69-16618.

Standard Book Number   7002   2203   0

FOR DONNA

 . . . . *to love her beyond words*
 . . . . *to like her beyond the enormity of life*
 . . . . *to share together in the joys of living*
 . . . . *to know her as strength and inspiration*
 . . . . *to listen to her voice . . . understand her smile*
 . . . . *to admire the depth of her patience . . . the tenderness of her care*
 . . . . *to cherish our eternal bond*
 . . . . *to see her as mother of Morgan, Mark, and Jill*
 . . . . *to have her as my wife*

are blessings from God that give my work and my writing meaning.

Foreword

Boards of trustees rose to prominence in the mid-1960's, although they had held court on the American campus since the founding of Harvard in 1636. A process of self-discovery took place among the brighter, more energetic trustees, coinciding with the national visibility given to the emerging, complex problems of higher education. In little over a decade higher education was transformed from small, elitist sanctuaries into large educational cities for the masses. This hyperactivity overloaded the traditional styles of management which had preserved stability on most campuses (presidents of institutions where administrative effectiveness first broke down being often referred to as "statesmen").

Many trustees now realize they can make more enduring and meaningful contributions to their alma maters if they give work and wisdom rather than wealth alone. But this means reexamining an old legend, handed down from one generation of self-perpetuating boards to another, that the charter of most colleges gives the governing board full power to *manage* the institution if it desires to do so.

This raises a thorny issue: How much power will the board take back? Since many governing boards might take back too many prerogatives too quickly—under pressure—administrators and trustees will have to debate this question phrased in the subjunctive mood. It is one thing for a president to know that a board may arbitrarily intrude on his administrative imperative upon occasion; it is quite another to know that such intrusions will be daily occurrences. In any event, the management style of most institutions of higher learning is changing.

Two facts about trustees hinder the proper reshuffling of authority and power on the campus: The average trustee is a business executive, and he graduated from college in the late 1920's. Colleges have long been able to disguise the fact that, organizationally, they have a corporate skeletal framework, but a mere fleshing out of the corporate skeleton will not provide sufficient answers to the problem of reinstituting effective administration on the campus: The decision-making process and political relationships differ markedly from those encountered in industrial organizations. And a greater share of "shared decision making" is the rallying cry today from faculty, students, and middle management. It is a cry that will have to be answered with responsibility, with honesty, and with soft words.

The challenge facing the college administrator is not how to find more innovative ways to keep the governing board neutralized, but how to make the governing board a knowledgeable partner in the administration of the academic enterprise. "Trustees are in a terrible bind now unless they have background in the education field or lengthy preparation by committee service," says Clark Kerr, former president of the University of California. "Their understanding is vital because the university now is one of the central institutions of society and thus it is vulnerable to attack. It's no longer an ivory tower that no one gives a damn about because it's somewhere on the periphery of society."

While *The Role of the Trustee* discusses *in toto* the subject of trusteemanship, it is because Orley Herron contends that you can take the businessman out of the trustee through in-service education programs that his book differs most importantly from other books on the subject. Several case studies and recommendations, applicable to a wide range of educational institutions, are presented, which are easily transferable to other institutions. If widely utilized, these techniques can go far in helping shape the administrative revolution now underway.

Depending upon whether the governing boards and the administrative teams in the power structure of higher education can develop new, effective relationships for strengthening institutions administratively and philosophically will hang the fate of higher education in America. It will determine whether the higher learning will continue in the groves or whether it will take place in the streets.

DENNIS W. BINNING
Editor-In-Chief
College and University Business
Chicago, Illinois

Preface

The recent campus demonstrations, student-rights disorders, enrollment growths, and knowledge explosions have brought new public attention to many college campuses.

The governing boards stand as the guardian and the guide of institutions of higher learning. How they exhibit their expertise will determine the destiny of higher education.

This book has been the outgrowth of the conviction that more should be done to help the trustee understand his multifaceted role. No book can give his role complete justice, but the present survey seeks to give an overview of his responsibility as the director of the educational enterprise. It is geared to assist the trustee in the performance of his duties. The book is also designed as a textbook and tool for administration personnel and for graduate students.

I wish to express my appreciation to many who directly and indirectly helped in the preparation of this book. Dr. Harold Miller of the University of Minnesota assisted me in Chapter 5, "Communication." Dr. Edward Ericson, a professor at Westmont College, Santa Barbara, California, and a trustee of another college, contributed in the area of student publications and philosophy of education found in Chapters 2 and 4.

Dr. Walter Johnson of Michigan State, my doctoral adviser and wonderful friend, originally motivated me to study trustees on my doctoral dissertation. In that study several people should be mentioned for thanks: Dr. Roger Voskuyl, past President of Westmont College and now Executive Director of the Council for the Advancement of Small Colleges; Dr. Al Hill, Former Executive Director of the Council for the Advancement of Small Colleges; and Dr. Ernest Boyer, Vice-Chancellor of University Wide Activities, State University of New York, all of whom greatly assisted in the preparation of a questionnaire to study trustees and also contributed in many other ways.

I am grateful to Mr. Bruce Bare, Chairman of the Board of Trustees of Westmont College, who contributed substantially in the section of the role of the chairman of the board in Chapter 4.

I also want to thank Dennis Binning, Executive Editor of the *College and University Business Journal*, who has been a good friend and advisor on the topic of trustees. The *Journal* he edits has given me an opportunity to voice variegated opinions in a column entitled "Governing Boards" . . . the reaction of their vast readership has given me invaluable insights. And I wish to acknowledge the excellent assistance received from the staff of International Textbook Company and its outstanding Education Editor, John Dugan, Jr.

Finally, I wish to thank my secretary Roberta Bowers, who labored with care and patience in the typing of the manuscript. Her diligence and enthusiasm are qualities that every secretary might emulate.

ORLEY HERRON

Terre Haute, Indiana
December, 1968

Contents

Introduction

The board of trustees is the single most important agency of an institution to state its case and to guide opinion. Few men in American history have ever had such magnificent opportunities or such weighing responsibilities as college trustees have today. In a world of rapid change the role of trustees takes on new urgency and increasingly becomes a channel for sophisticated talents. The world has mushroomed into a jet age and many a college governance board has not adapted to it. This book seeks to assist the trustee to understand his role, his commitment, and his responsibilities. The trustee needs to understand his role because of all the organizations in the world institutions of higher learning are the most dynamic—dynamic because they are in ferment intellectually, dynamic because they are rightfully committed to social improvement, and dynamic because they challenge hierarchies of thought and structure. Their social thrust which breeds controversy needs to be interpreted and reinterpreted to legislators, alumni, demonstrators, and other support groups. This mandate requires a charisma not often evidenced in staffs of today.

To meet the challenges of today modern trustees must be the most knowledgeable trustees of any generation. To better equip them for their role—this book is so designed.

The first chapter is an analysis of higher education as a system of social organization, and of the agencies that play the significant power roles in it.

The second chapter attempts to define the authority of trustees and to describe the implementation of that power. The American college is publicly chartered, and final authority for the institution rests with the governing board. In theory at least, their power is extremely wide. The style of management greatly affects a college or university. The governing board holds the key to a well-managed and high-moraled institution.

The third chapter is a crucial one because it discusses the role of the president. The board and president have the chartered responsibility to

demand that the decisions of their institution be consistent with its ultimate goals. Decisions apart from integrated goal commitments must be
carefully analyzed and reviewed before implementation.

The president is ever mindful in his role that he does not become so
involved in the day-by-day trivialities, such as paper reading, document
signing, and minor problem solving of faculty and students that he even-
tually loses his grasp on the major policies and items that should demand
his attention. A president could lose the respect of his colleagues by constant negotiation and attention to trivia when their major needs are so
pressing. Within the limitations of staff, time, and size of the campus the
president should know what is "happening" at his institution. For the most
part, he will rely on his delegated line officers to promote that flow of
communication.

The president and board have many difficult areas to administer.
One such sphere is to justify innovations. The board and president may
decide upon what is to be accomplished, but how to accomplish it can
be difficult. This is where the true test of leadership is validated.

The president is the institution's one officer who maintains constant
contact with the board. The president of many institutions has the power
to influence board selection. He must guide the selection of new members
to attract people of integrity, people with the capacity to learn, and
people who are willing to develop on the job.

There is no greater experience offered to citizens of our country than
to guide the destiny of higher education. Too often board members with
limited experience and narrow conceptions of higher education are
selected. The president must educate them to a level of deep dedication
and commitment to the goals of higher education and to the objectives
of their institution. The president must insure a trustee that his experience will be enlightening, exciting, and exulting. The trustee then will
be motivated to learn his responsibilities and the institution will recognize him for his generous donation of time and service.

The president is obligated to orient the board so that its members
do not become super egos to the institution. For example, a board member who is a doctor should not become a "super" doctor in the management of the medical school at the university he controls; and a board
member who is an educator should not become a "super dean" to the
institution he manages. Board members properly educated will listen to
the administrators, the deans, and the responsible officials. They will not
strive to become feudal lords or gods in their execution of authority.
The board must maintain a posture of listening and learning from the
professional educators they employ.

Many boards are so structured that politics enter the domain of higher education. A president can bridge the gap so that a check-and-balance system is established to purify the political interference.

Most boards have bylaws of their responsibilities and a clear delineation of the president's prerogatives. Misunderstandings can undermine good leadership and progress. A board should protect itself from underwritten styles of operation which hinder potentiality and capability.

The board and president stand as the leading statesmen of higher education. May they understand their roles well and lead with unswerving dedication.

The fourth chapter is devoted to analyzing ways of organizing the trustees for maximum effectiveness. Proper organization is extremely important and too often neglected.

The fifth chapter is geared to communication, and some proposals are submitted for consideration. Without adequate communication, a board and institution will chart different paths.

The sixth chapter is an analysis of case studies of in-service education programs found in various colleges across the country. These studies have received very good response in preliminary readings and give some practical hints to all institutions.

The seventh chapter ties in with the sixth and submits a plan on how to upgrade a board of trustees. This should be the theme of every college —upgrading their board. The last half of the chapter reveals ways of evaluating trustees.

Trustees are important and hold within their grasp the destiny of higher education. I trust this book will assist them in making their sojourn on the path of higher education a more enjoyable task.

CHAPTER I

The Power Structure in Higher Education

GOVERNING BOARDS AND THEIR ROLE IN THE SOCIALIZATION AND ORGANIZATION OF HIGHER EDUCATION

In any institution of higher learning the final authority for all affairs rests with the governing board. Its members are accountable for whatever matters they originate or approve, whenever and where-ever these matters have effect. This authority can be delegated but never eradicated. Delegation of authority is not avoidance or abdication, because the "buck" simply stops with the board of trustees. The trustees are ultimately responsible and will bear this yoke of responsibility to the highest courts of jurisprudence. The legality of their position may be questioned but it is secure. This is a precarious and somewhat difficult position for board members to assume. But as long as governing boards exist, they must expedite their prerogatives within the confines of the decision-making process charted for them. How they prescribe and present their powers of control will determine the environment upon which education transpires.

Veblen proposed to abolish all trustees. At some time during employment at an institution many persons may have uttered that theme—inwardly at least. Realistically speaking, however, it is doubtful that trustees will ever relinquish their constitutional power in governance. They are apparently here to stay, contrary to the wish of certain volatile groups.

If they are here to stay, it is important that they understand higher education as a powerful and persuasive system of social organization. Higher education has many facets, manifestations, models, and above all, many interpretations and perceptions. At times, nobody understands it, yet it may command either grudging respect or cynical lip-service. No brief discussion can do justice to the diversity of higher education; one can only point to the fact that there are approximately

1

2,400 institutions of higher learning, with thirty thousand or more trustees guiding their destiny.

There are those who regard higher education as the answer to the world's problems, or even grant it the status of an institution so noble that it deserves respect akin to reverence. Higher education should receive accolades merely because it does exist so that fair inquiry through the free minds of men can bring wisdom into human affairs.

On the one hand, higher education is an instrument of social privilege, a servant of the public and a perpetuator of the welfare of mankind. On the other hand, it is the guardian of the traditions of society and the laboratory of the future. It must, however, be bound by neither.

In some institutions, boards are struggling to maintain traditional standards in the face of dilution and dispersion of their effort.

Higher education needs direction, and the head of that procession is by authority the board of trustees. The boards must be alive with vision, so that the innovations necessary to the well-being of modern society can be initiated.

HIGHER EDUCATION AND SOCIETY

Institutions are bigger, better, and more prominent than ever before. They are destined to open to a large portion of individuals avenues of academic heights never before attained. This "orbiting of the mind" will bring new and difficult problems, and the board is vested to be equipped and ready for them. Activist students and a meddling or suspicious faculty confused as to authority represent a hint of what is to come. In a society of change, the status quo will be a livid fragmentation with constantly changing contours yet always directed at the academic community.

Colleges will and should differ one from the other. The board must understand correctly and clearly the differences. They may find incongruency and distortion in their analysis. But they must be able to observe their campuses as they are and how they ought to be.

Higher education has had a distinguished history and is well established. The board of trustees must be able to view the role of its institution in light of the new needs and the new diversities necessary for an ongoing society. Change in the social order must not permit change in the institution to be slow. Superior institutions will have superior trustees that can assimilate the needs and implement the strategies for change in modern society.

Trustees are to be leaders and sense the institutional changes necessary for their day-to-day operation.

In the final analysis trustees must recognize that the college and its society are inextricably related one to the other. College is an instrument of society, and from society's point of view has a utilitarian role. It is for this reason that certain of the problems of higher education are problems which it shares with or receives from society. The degree of expertise in meeting the needs of society will determine whether an institution will be mediocre or superior.

The board must realize that this self-consciousness is a factor that aggravates certain problems shared by the institution and society. It is responsible in part for the varying rates at which change occurs in the college and in society, and it is directly related to certain social problems caused by higher education.

Higher education is not an end in itself, but has the task of seeing that those who enter its halls are prepared for the whole fabric of higher education. If this is not its proper goal, education becomes a shaky bridge built upon rotten pilings.

The board must understand that higher education and culture or higher education and society are interdependent. Higher education by fact and by prescriptive right is a dominant force in our culture.

HIGHER EDUCATION AND PATTERNS OF ORGANIZATION

A board of trustees is aware that their college is characterized by group designs for living which may differ from the pattern found in the surrounding society.

The members of the college subculture know and typically subscribe to norms, values, and beliefs which differ from those of the surrounding culture but are part of the college subculture. Certain facilities, symbols, rituals, ceremonies, rewards, and sanctions are found to be unique or uniquely regarded within the college. The goals and norms of the college are not identical to those of the parent society, and the discrepancy between actual and ideal may be both different and differently regarded within the college. These differences can present dilemmas for a board of trustees.

A trustee is constantly made aware that a social and powerful structure exists within their college. There is a patterned system of relationships between and among status roles, such as trustee, president, professor, student, and administration. Some of these relationships are deemed significant by the members. They are defined carefully by norms, diffused throughout the membership by socialization, observed and evaluated as performed and preserved through techniques of social control which may involve the application of sanction against deviant behavior.

The board realizes that norms, however sanctioned, govern the use and selection by which instrumental, adaptive, integrative, and expressive goal-seeking activities are conducted.

A pattern of supersubordination can be evident within a college constituency—a hierarchical ranking system that includes faculty, staff, and students. There are patterns of authority upon which the board demands the focal point and around which have developed status roles occupied by college personnel and by students and alumni. Coupled with this are patterns of influence and noninstitutionalized coercive power which have developed around particular members. Some of these members may be very difficult for a board to command their respect and loyalty. Norms may govern an individual's passage from one status to another. Class, bonds of intimacy, affection, and common goals can link members together in an organization. The trustees should understand these norms and be able to unite the academic community through the institution's aims and objectives.

A college is not an isolated social system but rather an organized subsystem of a larger unit. Moreover, it is articulated with other social organizations through the process of systematic linkage, as when the initiative for change in the college may originate outside the college. The external forces promoting change may be technological, like the introduction of closed-circuit television and teaching machines, or they may be moral and represent a shift of norms in the parent society. They may stem from the fact of population growth, or from changes of educational expectations within the parent society. Systematic linkage is assured to some extent simply because members of the college are also members of and enter the college from the parent society. Turnover of personnel provides another means of articulation of systematic linkage with society.

The board of trustees and the president of the college perform status roles whose function is in large part that of assuring congruence in the organization. The question arises to what extent outside pressures are articulated by this group to influence the ends and means of a college.

COLLEGE SUBSYSTEMS OF ORGANIZATION

The boards must be acutely aware that in a single university or college organization there are many subsystems. There are various faculty peer systems, student-faculty systems, student systems, and administrative systems. There are overlapping memberships composed of all teaching personnel: research personnel, personnel posessing academic rank, all "profession" personnel (all professors of academic degree), professional nonacademic personnel, nonprofession personnel, nonacademic personnel, all nonacademic personnel, and all personnel occupying a given building or a particular department.

These social units constitute problems of boundary maintenance and systematic linkage. Through these processes, issues arise to whether certain people will be allowed membership in a particular social unit. These processes can stagnate policies of trustees if not carefully guarded.

In understanding the behavior of members of a college and a university, we must not forget that the complex of status roles, facilities, beliefs, and knowledge in higher education are all calculated and geared toward goals. From the point of view of society the board can visualize that these goals are disposed in terms of the motive, designs, aims and purposes of the members of the educational society, to whom the board is responsible. They are the chief administrators with the explicit ends-in-view of society and must be clear in that purpose.

In pursuit of specialized goals, the institutionalized actors within each college or university establish an organization and set forth specific purposes for their corporate behavior. This behavior presumably will satisfy society's expectations regarding purposes and behavior of the enterprises. Each enterprise or institution is managed by actors (boards) who occupy certain status roles. They plan, organize, staff, and control the enterprise and operations of their goal attaining adequacy. However, other members of society evaluate the college and university in terms of their needs, values, and beliefs. These societal expectations may become known to the actors (boards) within the colleges and might modify or confirm the organization and purposes of each institution.

INTERACTION WITHIN AN INSTITUTION

There are many emerging institutions within an institution. There are departmental interactions between the professor and the dean; the professor and another professor; and the professor and the student. The clubs, the associations, fraternities, sororities, athletic teams, residence halls, and religious groups all compose areas of interaction. These areas are all important to the board because they must have a cohesive relationship within the framework of their institution.

These interaction groups may bind themselves to powerful organizations, as when the faculty is affiliated with national or regional groups that can develop strong areas of confrontation for the board.

It is clear that patterns of interaction among college and univeristy personnel in their professional capacities transcend the boundaries of a single institution. Higher education is engulfed in a worldwide international pattern of interaction. The trustees must understand the inter- and intrarelationships because they motivate a group to function in a certain manner.

The board may permit the various groups to function interdependently but they must understand their flow of communication and its cause for their consequent ordering of behavior.

CONTROL OF AN INSTITUTION

There are informal and formal sanctions that clearly control an institution. The board makes explicitly clear their reasons for hiring, promotion, or firing a faculty member. The authorization of retention and suspension from a college are clearly a formal sanction. The informal sanctions can be the ones that control forcefully the charter and course of an institution. Yet within it all there is embedded a very definite ranking system.

In a particular university there is a board of trustees or a similar governing body, a president or chancellor, various deans, such as dean of the faculty, dean of students, dean of the business school, dean of education, etc. There may also be a vice-president and a business manager. Then within a particular department there is a hierarchy. The academic department has rankings such as assistant instructors, assistant professors, associate professors, and professors.

The trustees are the governing body of the institution. The president is directly responsible to this board. He is the legal spokesman of the institution. All other departments and personnel are under his jurisdicion with the trustees having final authority. The president distributes and delegates various authority to department heads, and they in turn are responsible for their own personnel. The hierarchical system finds some exceptions in the control and supervision of various departments. If a man is an instructor in an academic department, it does not mean he is responsible to the assistant professors, and that they in turn are responsible to the associate professor of that department. It means that his particular responsibility is with the department head unless otherwise delegated.

The board must strive to effect cohesiveness of all parts through a degree of impersonality and personal interaction so that the organization can function effectively.

One must remember that it takes time and careful study for the board to perceive the social systems of organization. Yet the board can be comforted in the knowledge that the specialization and diversion of labor of society, status roles of teacher, student, scientist, researcher, etc., are established and approximately defined. To the status role there is assigned a major share of the responsibility for activating the process of socialization and organization. Facilities are made available to and utilized by actors in these status roles. The complex of status roles, facilities, beliefs, knowledge, or goals is institutionalized and labeled "higher education." This complex is made manifest in a number of enterprises, which are labeled "colleges" and "universities" for which the board is responsible.

THE GROWTH OF HIGHER EDUCATION

The colleges and universities compose higher education and together comprise one of the most important institutions in our society. The expenditures funded for higher education grows each year and the end is not in sight. It is remarkable that in only three and a half centuries the American college could mushroom to the size and significance it now occupies. In the beginning the higher-education movement was small, limited, and geared to a very narrow curriculum. There were no multiversities like those we see today throughout the country. These early institutions are best illustrated by the colonial schools which were small liberal-arts colleges. They displayed a distinct patterning after Oxford and Cambridge and a strong influence from the French and German universities.

Harvard was founded in 1636 by the Puritan fathers and was governed by twelve overseers. They were six magistrates and six ministers who were chosen by the General Court to direct the school's affairs. The mission for education was limited and their student enrollment small.

In 1693, the College of William and Mary was founded to supply the Anglican Church with a seminary for ministers so that the Gospel could be spread to the new world. The school was designed to reach the western Indians with the Christian faith as well as to train young people with good manners and good letters. The Reverend James Blair served as head of the school until 1743. Located in Virginia, it was the only institution of higher learning in the South during the entire colonial period.

Seeing a need for another institution comparable to Harvard, ten ministers accquired a charter from the General Court of Connecticut establishing Yale in that colony on October 9, 1701. The charter was granted so that young people could be trained for employment in church and civil affairs. Elihu Yale gave money so that the first building could be completed.

In 1746 the College of New Jersey was founded by the Presbyterian leadership to establish a ministerial training school for future clergymen. The institution changed its name to Princeton University and during the early years served the middle colonies and the south. Kings College, now Columbia University, was initiated through the efforts of the local Church of England and started in 1754.

In 1764 Brown University came into existence in Providence, Rhode Island, though first founded in New Jersey as a ministerial training school.

Rutgers—founded by the Reformed Dutch in 1766, and Dartmouth—established in 1769 by the Congregational Church, followed similar patterns established by the other colonial institutions.

These eight pioneer institutions set the stage for what was to follow in the design for higher learning in the United States.

In those early years the influence of the church was extremely predominant and their control was tightly administered.

INFLUENCES IN HIGHER EDUCATION

From the early beginnings of American higher education certain forces have played a significant impact in its structure. This influence has been profound and continues to penetrate deeply in the design and nature of education. For want of a better term these forces might be called the "power structure" of higher education. They move, command, and guide the direction of an institution by one means or another. Their sturcture is sometimes vague but their influence is vital. The major forces in the scope of an institution are the faculty, the alumni, the constituency, the student, the administration, and the trustee.

A very neat flow chart could be established placing the trustee on top but such a diagram would not reveal truly and operationally what actually occurs. The other forces have presented some powerful countervailing agencies and hold a substantial pinnacle in the power structure of an institution.

Boards of Trustees and Faculty Relationships

The faculty represents the most powerful force within the structure of responsibility academically. The faculty members are the bulwark and foundation stone of the academic enterprise. They are the genius of the academic program and can make it move successfully or stagnate it beyond repair. The faculty is a curious animal and must be understood properly and wisely. Many a board member has erred in the judgment of a faculty member, with consequences that have hindered the progress of the institution. No effort should be left untried to ensure the proper selection, recruitment, and representation of the academic faculty. They hold the key to either mediocrity or strength within an institution.

The faculty members have received many a scar in the quest for proper recognition within higher education. These scars have won the battles of guaranteed employment, academic freedom, curriculum selection, and evaluation by their peer committees. They are careful in the guardianship of these rights and greatly suspicious when the board moves in the direction of their areas of discipline.

It is extremely difficult for a faculty member to accept the decisions of a board when he may be aware that the various board members know little or nothing about the discipline areas in which that faculty member teaches.

This is not the total picture of faculty perception of trustee power but it does illustrate an attitude found within the academic power structure. An attitude that is quite prevalent on numerous college campuses.

The Role of the Professor

The role of the professor or faculty member has changed substantially since early colonial days. In early times he was a generalist, but with such innovations as the secularization of education, the rise of the state-supported institutions, and rapid developments in science and technology, he has become a specialist. Additional factors have been the rise of the elective system, the increase in the natural sciences, and the rise of the universities and multiversities.

Professional societies and organizations have sprung up which grant the faculty member new and collective power, unknown before. These organizations gain the loyalty of the faculty because of their homogeneous discipline identity and give him a leverage that becomes quite penetrating to a board of trustees.

Academic freedom has proven and will continue to be a dilemma for many a trustee. The spirit of inquiry by its very nature requires questioning and investigation that could lead to controversy for a trustee board. Academic freedom is not a license for irresponsibility but an invisible contract binding the faculty and trustee together in the search for truth. Freedom requires confidence and its implementation requires discretion. The board may need the wisdom of Solomon to exercise the correct prerogatives in dealing with problems of academic freedoms that may arise. Improper infringement must be corrected quickly and firmly. The trustee should beware of those who, in the name of scholarship and learning, peddle simple solutions to life's complex problems. These are the people who have come to the road's end of their education, having failed to realize that understanding is a never-ending process, not a destination.

Faculty members are willing to permit the professionals to manage the financial and plant affairs of the university because of their multi-faceted and detailed vectors.

Boards of trustees should permit faculties to elect representatives to handle the academic policies · and decisions they require. The academic area is their life and they are jealous in the administration of it. The board should be careful about interfering in this area.

As an institution grows the trustee must be critically cognizant of the faculty members' needs and desires. They are not prima donnas who are to be coddled, but professionals desirous of the best standards of ethics, environment, and programs to be displayed on their campus. Faculties and governing boards can draw imaginary battle lines which are not healthy for the growth of higher education. Faculties and trustees must be statesmen in their various levels of leadership.

There is a middle ground of respect and honor to be achieved between faculty and trustee. Their background bias may differ but their aims should agree in the actualization of the educational goals of their institution. They are builders together and must not let misunderstanding and indifference destroy the fiber of respect and honor necessary for their well-being.

Though faculty members may only see their role through their professional discipline, the board must raise high the goals and objectives of the academic enterprise so that it becomes a cooperative venture. Never a command or coercive course.

The Students

If faculties present an enigma to boards of trustees, the students do even more so. They are the reasons for the existence of an institution and are a vital element in the power structure. Their role can have a deep effect and bearing on the destiny of the establishment. A trustee cannot insulate himself from a student's role or his determinations. Most trustees do not understand the modern-day student, yet their institution exists to educate him for society.

The student of today is more sophisticated socially and intellectually then ever before. He is an eyewitness and participant in the most advanced era in human history. The advancement has not lessened pressures but increases them. The flame of academia is rising higher on students and many are falling under its influence. Students do feel the pressures and are choosing some startling alternatives—not excluding suicide—to relieve them.

The quest for student power can and sometimes does disrupt the orderly process of education. A trustee board must have the channels of communication open so that they know the student and his needs. Figuratively a board may be sitting on a powder keg and be caught completely off balance when an outbreak occurs.

The board must learn to act, not react to students. Students may become overanxious and greatly concerned over issues affecting them. The board must establish the proper machinery to deal with their needs. Their relationship must be based on reasonable, rational, and relevant issues. Their attitudes should exhibit openness, frankness, and respect. Students that are misguided, misused, and forgotten can be pretty hard for any governing body to cope with.

A vast majority of students are between the ages of 17–21, an age in which many drives and needs are seeking expression. The expression of the desires must be displayed in acts that are not in the best interest of an institution nor are they conducive to the students' well-being. Discipline, including suspension, is not always the best teacher; nor is fear the wisest educator.

Proper agencies and services should be established to deal with some of the adjustment needs of students. An institution cannot tell a student to leave his problems at home. A board must permit students to come as they are academically qualified and must promote the necessary agencies for their satisfactory adjustment to college.

Because many campuses have grown to sizes of fairly large cities, the board must expect some problems similar to those of a city-complex from its students. The institution is not a rehabilitation center—it is a community of adventuring scholars.

Student representation can be used wisely and judiciously for the smooth operation of an institution. Don't be hesitant to grant student government the power of representation. Let them be the channels of student leadership on campus. Splinter and reactionary groups should not be given prominence and privilege in the channels of communication. Although they need to be heard, they must learn the responsibility of the elective representatives—certainly in the halls of learning. Trustees and administrators are skating on thin ice when they let groups emerge and give them power without being cleared through the normal procedural methodology for institutional valuation. Splinter and reactionary groups will constantly arise and may at times be healthy for the fertile and active collegiate mind. Some campuses, however, have let them grow without sanction and direction to the point of no return. I refer in particular to militant groups that do not have the institution's aims and objectives as their basis.

Power can be the greatest force for good or evil on the campus. Examine a student group's philosophy of power. It will be their guide on how they function and how they expedite their program. If the students are to be the leaders of our society, let them learn the democratic checks-and-balance system well so it can be internalized in their programming. Students, however, should not be brainwashed with administrative propaganda; but through reason and negotiation they should learn the objectives of the educational process of their campus.

Remember there is a fine line between hypocrisy and diplomacy, and too often administration and govering boards are guilty of hypocrisy.

Students need representation. Make sure it is channeled through the administration, and guided with the objectives of your institution and the goals of higher education.

There are many such groups of student population which need attention and understanding. The late adolescent is like a ship looking for a harbor, or an island in a sea of hostility.

Let the students know and learn that trustees are not the Gods of Olympus but are co-workers in the venture for academic excellence.

A trustee board should provide within its scope that the experiences in the classroom and without are contributing to the educational process. Because a great deal of learning takes place outside the classroom, each building that is contructed and each individual that is hired is contributing in some way to the student welfare and education. Students are important—treat them accordingly.

The Alumni

The alumni can be a powerful force to their particular institutions. Some institutions feel their influence far more profoundly than do others.

Administrators and trustees should not be surprised when alumni groups bear down upon them. Though the graduate may be actively involved in a progressive business or other endeavor, he may feel protectively toward his alma mater. This spirit is part of the nostalgia that automatically becomes internalized in graduates who are strongly attached to their school. Many of the private institutions develop strong and loyal alumni groups who become quite difficult to handle unless guided by a thorough, cohesive program designed with cooperative ventures involving administrators and alumni participants. Trustees do have an obligation to their graduates, but this obligation requires a responsibility to keep them informed of the progress and state of the institution.

Trustees should not condescend to the powerful influence of the alumni if they feel an opposite opinion regarding the decision-making process. Alumni will always be concerned, as they should be. Don't back away from a direction, a position, or an alternative when it is

DANA, E. H. "Why College Trustees?" *Journal of Higher Education*, XVIII (May 1947), pp. 259–262.

DELANY, WILLIAM. "The Development and Decline of Patrimonial and Bureaucratic Administration," *Administrative Science Quarterly* (March 1963), pp. 458–501.

FRANKEL, CHARLES (ed.). *Issues in University Education.* New York: Harper, 1959.

GAUSS, CHRISTIAN. "Education," in Harold E. Stearns (ed.), *American Now.* New York: Literary Guild, 1938.

GLENNY, LYMAN A. *Autonomy of Public Colleges: The Challenge of Coordination,* New York: McGraw-Hill, 1959.

GREER, SCOTT. *Social Organization.* New York: Random House, 1955.

GROSS, NEAL. "The Sociology of Education," in Robert K. Merton et al., *Sociology Today.* New York: Basic Books, 1959.

HAVEMANN, ERNEST, and PATRICIA SALTER WEST. *They Went to College.* New York: Harcourt, 1952.

HAVINGHURST, ROBERT J. "The Governing of the University," *School and Society* (March 20, 1954), pp. 81–86.

HOFSTADTER, RICHARD, and C. DEWITT HARDY. *The Development and Scope of Higher Education in the United States.* New York: Columbia U.P., 1955.

———, and WALTER P. METZGER. *The Development of Academic Freedom in the United States.* New York: Columbia U.P., 1955.

HOLLINGSHEAD, BYRON S. *Who Should Go to College?* with a chapter by Robert J. Havinghurst and Robert R. Rodgers. New York: Columbia U.P., 1952.

HOMANS, GEORGE C. *The Human Group.* New York: Harcourt, 1950.

HUNTER, FLOYD. *Community Power Structure.* Chapel Hill: U. of North Carolina Press, 1953.

HUTCHINS, ROBERT MAYNARD. *The Higher Learning in America.* New Haven: Yale U.P., 1936.

JACOB, PHILIP E. *Changing Values in College: An Exploratory Study of the Impact of General Education in Social Sciences on the Values of American Students.* New York: Harper, 1957.

KELLEY, EARL C. *Education for What Is Real.* New York: Harper, 1947.

KNIGHT, DOUGLAS M. (ed.). *The Federal Government and Higher Education.* Englewood Cliffs, N.J.: Prentice-Hall (Spectrum), 1960.

KRUTCH, JOSEPH WOOD, et al. *Is the Common Man Too Common?* Norman, Oklahoma: U. of Oklahoma Press, 1954.

LAZARSFELD, PAUL F., and WAGNER THIELENS, JR., with DAVID RIESMAN, *The Academic Mind.* New York: Free Press, 1958.

LOOMIS, CHARLES P. *Social Systems.* Princeton, N.J.: Van Nostrand, 1960.

McCONNELL, T. R., and PAUL HEIST. "Do Students Make the College?" *College and University* (Summer 1959), pp. 442–452.

McGRATH, EARL J. "The Control of Higher Education in America," *Educational Review* (April 1936), pp. 356–372.

MEAD, MARGARET (ed.). *Cultural Patterns and Technical Change.* New York: New American Library, 1955.

MILLET, JOHN D. *The Academic Community.* New York: McGraw-Hill, 1962.

PARSONS, TALCOTT. *The Structure of Social Action.* New York: Free Press, 1949.

———, and EDWARD A. SHILS (eds.). *Toward A General Theory of Action.* Cambridge: Harvard U.P., 1951.

President's Commission on Higher Education. *Higher Education for American Democracy*, Washington, D.C.: Department of Health, Education, and Welfare, 1947.

RIESMAN, DAVID. *Constraint and Variety in American Education*, Lincoln: U. of Nebraska Press, 1956.

————, with NATHAN GLAZER and REUL DENNY. *The Lonely Crowd*. (Yale U.P., 1950). New York: Doubleday and Co., Inc., Anchor Edition, 1953.

RUML, BEARDSLEY, and DONALD H. MORRISON. *Memo to a College Trustee*. New York: McGraw-Hill, 1959.

TEWKSBURG, DONALD E. *The Founding of American Colleges and Universities Before the Civil War with Particular Reference to the Religious Influences Bearing Upon the College Movement*. Teachers College, Columbia University Contribution to Education. No. 543, New York: Bureau of Publications, Teachers College, Columbia University, 1932.

VEBLEN, THORSTEIN. *The Higher Learning in America*. New York: Sagamore Press, 1957.

WILSON, LOGAN. *The Academic Man*. New York: Oxford U.P., 1942.

WOODBURNE, LLOYD S. *Faculty Personnel Policies in Higher Education*. New York: Harper, 1950.

WRISTON, HENRY M. *Academic Procession*. New York: Columbia U.P., 1959.

CHAPTER 2

The Power and Prerogatives of Trustees

Rufus C. Harris,[1] former president of Tulane University, has stated that the most important single factor in higher education is the board of trustees.

The point is well taken, for it is the college board that selects the administration, assembles a faculty, and in a myriad of ways shapes the campus, both physically and philosophically. While the wisdom of such sweeping power often is challenged, the fact remains that at the typical American college it is the governing board that directs both present-day progress and the long-range destiny of the institution.

Charged with so sweeping a mandate, the work of the board of trustees becomes remarkably complex. The college's governing body wrestles with building codes, housing arrangements, wills and bequests, strategies of fund raising, student affairs, and government contracts. Above all, the board must see to it that all subordinate functions mix in a way that ultimately serves the institution's educational needs.[2]

The ideals of the faculties, the quality of the teaching, and the college's adaption to the current needs of society depend largely, as Raymond Hughes so aptly noted, on the board of trustees.[3]

The trustees hold within their constitutional powers the authority to make all decisions regarding their institution. Rightly or wrongly, the power center of a majority of institutions of higher learning still remains in the hands of a small corporate body called trustees or board of regents. Although the primary role of the college is education, by and large few trustees hold degrees above the B.A. degree. And yet these boards make some of the most significant decisions regarding educational policy.

Trustees are legally responsible for the institution they serve. They

---

[1] Orley R. Herron and Ernest L. Boyer, "What Small Colleges Want—and What They Get—in Trustees," *College and University Business Journal*, Vol. 42, No. 3 (March 1967), pp. 77–79.
[2] *Ibid.*
[3] *Ibid.*

can be sued as a corporate body and are legally endowed to handle the financial affairs of the institution.

The trustees are incorporated by law to act as the trustees for the owners of the institution. The owners of the public institution are the tax payer and for private institution the designees.

BASIC DUTIES AND POWERS OF TRUSTEES

1. The board has the power and duty to manage and control the particular institution or institutions it is constitutionally authorized to control.

2. They must succeed to and continue to exercise control of all records, books, papers, equipment and supplies, and all lands, buildings, and other real and personal property now or hereafter belonging to or assigned to the use of their institution, and shall have and exercise control of the use, distribution and disbursement of all funds, appropriations, gifts granted for the use, benefit, support and maintenance or capital outlay expenditure of their institution of higher learning.

3. The board is empowered with the affairs of the department and the conduct of the libraries and laboratories, the care of residence halls, buildings and grounds, the business methods and arrangements of accounts and records, the organization of the administrative plan of each institution, as well as the establishment of new courses of study, new departments, and new functions and activities in the institution, including all other matters incident to the proper functioning of the institution.

4. The board has the power to make any adjustment it thinks necessary between various departments or other related areas within the institution.

5. The board may also appoint a secretary and elect a chairman to assist in the accomplishment of the purposes for which the board was established.

6. The board is empowered to establish minimum standards of achievement as a prerequisite for admission into the institution and to determine who shall be privileged to enter, to remain in, or to graduate from any of the institutions.

7. The board has the authority to adopt bylaws and regulations, not repugnant to the contribution and laws of the state and not inconsistent with the object for which the institution was created, for the proper supervision and control thereof.

8. If it is a state university, the board has the power to conduct all relationships and negotiations between the state legislature and its various committees and the several institutions.

9. The board may adopt and use in the authentication of its acts an official seal.

10. If public, the board shall keep minutes and records of its proceedings which shall be open for inspection by any citizens of the state.

11. The board shall prepare the proper reports to validate all receipts and disbursements of the institution.

12. The board shall elect the head of the institution and to contract with faculty and staff.

13. The board has the power to terminate the contract of any employee at any time for malfeasance, inefficiency, insubordination, and improper conduct.

14. The board shall serve as the Final Court of Appeal at the institution for faculty, staff, students, and administration.

15. The board has the power to grant honorary degrees to those designated.

These are the broad duties of most governing boards in the United States. The specific expediting of the duties will vary from one institution to another.

POWER PREROGATIVES

The board deals mainly in three areas: (1) policy formation, (2) setting of long-range objectives, and (3) long-range strategic planning.

The board should not initiate policy but devise the structure to create policy. Although the board is the highest level of organization for policy authorization, experience has shown that delegation is the wisest course in policy formulation. In the area of long-range objectives and planning, the board charts the course. It gives the directional boundaries upon which the institution will journey. The ends and means of the journey will be evidenced in the pattern of delegation and advisement.

The board solves the problem of delegation by:

1. Clearly stating its prerogatives in decision making at the board level.

2. Establishing an executive organization and appointing the president of the institution to head the institutional operation.

3. Delegating to the president and his executives the powers they need to do the job.

The charter and bylaws should make it clear and specific what the board cannot delegate.

The board in their organization for delegation must define the duties and responsibilities of those people and agencies given the delegation.

The degree to which any board should delegate becomes an institutional decision which only that board can formulate. The pattern of delegation needs constant revision to validate the current climate of the campus and society.

What the board does not delegate to itself it delegates to others deliberately or by default. Confusion does not have to dominate a board relative to policy power and implementation.

The board having delegated certain powers provides the advice and consultation to management on matters within the scope of its responsibility. It offers constructive advice and criticism, and promotes actions by the president and his subordinates which are in the best interests of the institution. Whether under conditions of maximum or minimum delegation, the advice and counsel of board members are important in the conduct of institutional affairs.

The board is the body that assumes the resolute implementation and actualization of the goals of the institution.

The clear expression of duty is derived from the fact that the board of directors is corporately liable in the instances of failure to manage prudently the assets of the institution.

The style of delegation of authority is to be resplendent with evaluation, review, and projection. The board is responsible that the available indicators, broad-based, judgments, periodic reevaluation, and alternative plans are within its available grasp to determine decisions. Its task is to mobilize the institution with its resources to its greatest capability. The success or failure of its control will be clearly evident.

The managerial skill of the board needs to be extensive if it is to contribute significantly to the process of educational decision making.

THE MANAGEMENT AND CONTROL OF INSTITUTIONS

Once the charter of incorporation is finalized and authorized, the board is legally in business. How the board uses that power is left to its own choosing. The removal of Clark Kerr as president of the University of California in 1966, no matter what position one desires to maintain on that subject, stirred many boards of trustees to tighten their grip on their respective institutions. This reaction awakened some boards from the apathy of the "rubber stamp" philosophy to the demonstration of powerful, decisive, and ever-threatening positions of the part of administrators. This "mass identification" of boards with the California structure may have been just a passing phase. There will always be incidents that light the spark of "mass identification." When such a renaissance occurs, it must not be dismissed lightly. It is the role of the board to exercise "trusteemanship" and it is the task of the institution and public to see that their management of power is not improperly utilized. Unwise implementation of control by trustees could reverse the progress of the institution to a point from which it could never recover.

It is paramount that a board understand the nature and personality of the institution it serves. The nature of the institution may necessitate a type of management, control, and priority different from that of others.

Dictatorships have no place in the strategy of control on a campus. Strong authoritarian control can weaken the fiber of administrative leadership so vital to the progress of an institution. It is important that each trustee examine his philosophy of power and then determine if it is proper, beneficial, and strengthening to the academic enterprise. If a board member is appointed because of a bias that he has demonstrated to the board, the institution may be in trouble.

In the management of an institution a board will be faced with receiving many types of information both good and bad, valid and invalid. A board must guard against being trapped with judgments or decisions on matters that are not perfectly clear and reliable. The board must always make sure there is proper time and understanding to validate the information presented before enacting a decision relative to it.

Rumors have a way of mushrooming. Boards of trustees that permit suspicion, distrust, and inflexibility to run rampant throughout an institution will soon become only the caretakers of a graveyard of learning. Such a university or college cannot survive in a world that once again needs strength, trust, and vision.

The board, in the exercise of control, must exhibit dynamic leadership. Leadership is the outward expression of an inward conviction lived in a realistic experience. To be a leader one must have followers. The ironic situation is that people will be led only to the degree that they want to be led. The board must lead them beyond that degree.

The properly skilled board will be able to attract an extremely qualified president as the chief executive officer. He, in turn, will be able to recruit a top-level team to manage the institution. This "first team" will be able to select, recruit, and identify the faculty and other members necessary to balance the quality of excellence. The constituency will identify readily with such excellence and contribute liberally to its progress. The alumni will be grateful for such quality and will encourage highly trained and motivated students to seek admission. The students will then assist in creating an environment where the process of learning and the objectives of the institution can best be achieved.[4]

There is a great need for a redefinition of the role and the necessity of a corporate group called "trustees." Many trustees perform poorly because they are selected illogically, trained sporadically, and communicated with irregularly. Thus they misunderstand their role in light of the aims and objectives of their institution. A board of trustees that understand its role and exercises its responsibility will develop an institution where education can be exhibited at its finest.

[4] Orley R. Herron, "Critical Observations On the Power and Prerogatives of Trustees," *College and University Business*, Vol. 42, No. 5 (May 1967), pp. 70–71.

Colleges and universities that desire to make a significant impact on knowledge must have a board of trustees that is educationally and managerially "daring" enough to meet the demands for the future of the educative program.

A well-trained, carefully selected, continuously oriented and involved board will make the critical decisions necessary for excellence in its institution.

Most trustee boards are more cognizant of public and constituent opinion. Therefore, many of their decisions are geared to public acceptance rather than for their unadulterated educational value. This is extremely sad and more than not quite detrimental to the growth of a school. If the institution is to lead society it must be careful to determine the direction it deems best to take. The role of the institution is to lead, not to be led. The board must always make that distinction. The educational process by its very nature demands tension, stress, experimentation. These things can lead to difficulty, but that is part of the price we must pay for new and conquered educational pursuits.

The trustee must have the overriding philosophy that quality education is vital and important for the ongoing of society. This philosophy permits diversity and flexibility to infiltrate schools of higher learning.

The trustee seeks not to gain by self-aggrandizement or personal financial influence.

With this philosophy, a board will make sure the institution is well managed. The search for decision in policy matters will rest upon the most reliable and relevant information available. The decisions then will be based upon the best interests of the school and its role in society.

The display and exercise of control in the management of an institution has no peer.

Trustees spend much of their time on fiscal and plant development. Because of attention to these concerns, hasty decisions are sometimes made regarding educational policy, which creates a wide underlying gap.

The board must decide the scope of its responsibility and must develop methods to care for that responsibility. This is where delegation of authority is suitable. There are some areas of management that can only be expedited by the board. There are other dimensions that can be easily delegated. The board should not become involved in mundane policy decisions which can be better handled through delegated administration. It ought to capture the top-policy decisions as its priority and not become involved in the small details of day-by-day internal affairs. It is mandatory that trustees avoid duplication and overlapping of responsibilities. Trustees need to be able to delegate and give confidence and authority to the person to whom it is delegated.

Do not let the delegation be halfhearted or permit your administrator to stand on the precipice of default. The wiser choice is to delegate when you can and then establish the proper channels of implementation and follow-through.

In all matters of management and control the board has a choice. How it exercises that prerogative of choice is a test of its ability to lead.

FINANCIAL AND PLANT MANAGEMENT

All institutions require money, and the management of the financial affairs is one of the crucial areas of trusteemanship. Most institutions are multimillion-dollar enterprises. The distribution and disbursement of the funds require careful analysis by the board.

Adequate accounting procedures must be established to maintain the most sophisticated balance of the monies.

The board has the prerogative to deal with the minute accounting of budgetary items or the prerogative to handle only the major items. Most important, the board has the final authorization of the budget. The budget design and implementation controls the nature of the institution for a particular year. Within the budget appropriations may be decisions on whether to increase salaries of faculty or give attention to another item. It is to be hoped that a board is not faced too often with that decision.

Money is related to power. The board must be careful that those who are delegated with the disbursement of monies do not become the power block within the institution. It is true that in some colleges and universities the business manager really runs the college, not the chief executive. This arrangement is quite natural, since many board members are businessmen and find an easy and automatic relationship with the man in charge of finance. The board should guard against this familiarity because it is not in the best interests of the academic community. Examine the administrative structure and determine who is really in control!

The board is chartered to advise, review, and approve the annual or biennial budget. There are few institutions that have an easy margin of reserve when it comes to the monies available for their institution. Major fund-raising programs that have been so prevalent across the country have not answered the financial needs of the school. A board's duty is to see that the administration hires a wise and capable development officer. A high-level development officer can bring millions of dollars in funds to an institution. His wisdom, tact, and ability can make the difference financially in an institution. These men must be paid well because they are key officers. They should not receive more salary than the top academic officers. Many a strained feeling has occurred in institutions that permitted the development officer to secure a salary above the academic dean or similar academic executives.

Each faculty member as well as department head is jealous of his budget. The board will have to rely upon the delegated administrative officers to interpret the needs of the department accurately to the board. The board must ever be alert to detect favoritism in budget allocations. Too often the people that campaign the longest and loudest receive the lion's share of the budget. The board is obligated to decipher such irresponsibility. Careful and thorough procedures had best be established for budget preparations, review, approval, and allocation. Don't "major in minors" in budget analysis—major in the top and large areas of priority.

CONSTRUCTION

The board is compelled to establish priority in the building program. A balanced building program is essential. Board members have bias to certain areas and they must be careful not to permit such bias to prevail in building commitments. The board may set short- and long-range goals for each building. The site, drawings, and cost require review. Means of funding a building must be clearly understood and programmed. A benefactor may desire to fund a building which is fifth on the priority; this is where flexibility is permitted. A building should "fit" the particular campus. A building constructed on one campus may be out of place on another. The style of architecture ought to reflect the environment the board wishes to establish and above all, capitalize on the natural setting and protect the God-given landscapes you have. Errors in construction are multimillion-dollar mistakes. Few colleges can afford the extravagance of such architectural wrongdoings.

A board will decide if a campus will reflect a familiar design, motif, and architecture or if it will reflect diversity and individuality.

Every building can reflect the opinions, judgments, and recommendations of the staff that will be housed in the structure. Every building must complement the educational program whether or not those that will live in and supervise the new building participate in its formulation. They can assist the architects and board tremendously.

The best approach to a building program is to secure an architectural firm to work out a campus master plan. This plan will be modified each year and may be reviewed completely every seven years. No campus should be without a master plan, and it is the board's job to protect a campus against that possibility. Although flexible, the master plan will be a guideline for all. Faced with goals of master plans, institutional objectives, and educational philosophy a board must manage to give its best administrative guidance.

ACADEMIC AND CURRICULAR GOVERNANCE

Boards cannot plunge wholeheartedly into the total spectrum of academic planning and curriculum control. Faculty members will not surrender the control of the curriculum, and to seek such control is highly unadvisable and misguided. The board has the legal power to do so, but it may be a fatally functional error.

The academic administration should be delegated to insure the proper development and innovation of academic policy. If the board has selected the proper man to lead the institution, then the institution will not steer a faculty course academically. The board can and should react to the curriculum suggestions. However, it should only react—not initiate such undertakings. It must respond to poor organization and improper decision, and must veto unwise policies. How it reacts may be judged by the accrediting agencies. The board asks questions which may be embarrassing academically but it does so in order to serve as part of the checks-and-balance system within the academic confines.

The faculty has organized to put pressure on governing bodies at many institutions. The establishment and strengthen of the academic senate has been the answer to academic governance. The senate is a single, comprehensive body and usually is fairly representative. In many cases, the senate is composed of all eligible faculty members who elect a council or some similar body to conduct the business of the internal academic organization. The board needs to recognize an academic senate or its equivalent with full governing powers in academic policy. If it proves to be ineffective, then some other form of representation will come into being and the board can permit its creation.

The academic domain in all probability had best be left to the academic professional. The board can always be the body for final review and authorization regarding academic policy.

To function smoothly, academic governance must be a clearly delegated and authorized prerogative. If a board chooses to handle the intiative of academic policy, this will be a twenty-four-hour-a-day assignment. The key to it is the willingness or unwillingness upon the part of the board, the faculty, or the administration in developing appropriate and constructive patterns of shared responsibility based on cooperation. Each has a mutual stake in the educational process and its outcome.

RUBBER-STAMP PHILOSOPHY

There is the evil of developing a cozy alliance with the administration where objectivity completely erodes. All too frequently inadequate areas are covered up, cancerous crises glossed over, and poor administrators carefully concealed. A board must probe with persistence, not meddle in order to find out what is going on! The word "why" should be used frequently. A rubber-stamp board is a handicap in these difficult times.

The trustees have an obligation to keep everyone on his toes. This type of relationship can be healthy, intellectually honest, and invigorating for the academic community. It is not a Big Brother or Gestapo system but a highly qualified methodology to keep the top administration from occasional misjudgment and from being led down a blind alley.

A rubber-stamp philosophy causes an institution to stagnate and regress. The board should cultivate a strategy of insightful questioning and depth analysis in studying reports sent to it for authorization. Board members are not second-guessers but delineators of the difference between good answers and merely plausible ones.

Top administrators will appreciate a board that is careful in seeing that the college affairs are satisfactorily conducted. There are routine recommendations that need little review or analysis. The board's concern and attention are with major policy decision, an area where it cannot afford to be a rubber stamp. With this approach it can develop the ability to persistently ask the right questions and to admit error, duplication, and passivity. Disturbing trends will be ignored by the board if it does not have an open channel to the institution to learn what is really transpiring. If the board is adept then it will make sure that unwise suggestions and faulty leadership do not abound.

TRUSTEES MUST BE FLEXIBLE

Total rigidity in an academic community is the kiss of death to academic growth. Trustees must be able to support imaginative and new departures when they may contradict traditional policy or ideology. This type of flexibility demands sophistication, courage, and strength. They are coadventurers in the discovery of new knowledge. This quest requires a new sense of daring and risk-taking which may not have been evidenced before.

The board has the prerogative of maintaining the institution in the status quo of past generations or of vigorously defending new innovations, methodologies, and approaches. The board should be willing to accept the consequence of innovation. Rigid boards that stoically hold to tradition may be left at the station in the academic future. The trustee is the link and guardian of the passage from the old frontier to the new. He is obligated to put on the armor of strength to wage the battle in the struggle for new knowledge. The board is the reconciliation of tradition and the new world. Its task is not to permit decadence through rigidity but to encourage learning through innovation. It had best be committed to the spirit of free inquiry and its obligations.

STUDENT AFFAIRS

Admissions

The board determines the admission policy. This requires that it be consistent with the objectives and philosophy of the institution. Admission procedures need be carefully spelled out and followed. The admission policy of each institution is a prerogative given to the institution. The board should provide an admissions policy that clearly distinguishes the characteristics and expectations of students of certain persuasion. Such a preference, however, should be clearly and publicly stated. The board must not permit a student to be barred on the basis of race. The board determines within the limits of its facilities and services the number of the student population they can enroll. Within these specifications qualified students should be enrolled.

The board members may have friends whose children they would like to see enrolled in their particular institution. The board members should not exert pressure or influence to secure an enrollment space for borderline candidates even though they be close friends. This style of board interference is power politics and weakens the objective policy of the admissions director.

The board may permit itself to have a quota of board student recommendations. This simply means that a board may choose the alternative of having one or two students as their prerogative to admit each year. This method would not embarrass the admissions officer.

Procedural Standards for Discipline

The board stands as the final authority in matters of discipline. Only the board can expel a student, and this expulsion prohibits him from returning to the institution. The board should ensure that its institutional powers do not inhibit the intellectual, emotional, and personal development of the students. This development is often promoted by their exercise of the rights of citizenship both on and off campus.

Governing boards are responsible for providing procedural fairness in the administration of discipline. Disciplinary action may vary with the severity of the offense. Safeguards in the proceedings must be built in to allow the legal rights of both student and board to be clearly ascertained.

The board has an obligation to have its institution clarify the standards of behavior which it considers essential to the fulfillment of its objectives and goals.

The behavioral expectations should be published and explained to the student population. Violations of these standards must be clearly explained and must be consistent with the institution's aims and educational philosophy. The disciplinary procedures relative to infraction can be publicized after formulation in the student handbook or similar publication.

Students can be invited by the board and administration to assist in the establishment of the proper behavioral expectations, infractions, and disciplinary proceedings necessary for their unique campuses.

In the hearing and investigation of the student's conduct the procedural due-process rule must be followed. The board should review its judicial disciplinary process yearly to ensure that the principles are up to date.

The investigation of conduct requires protection of student rights against unauthorized search of students' rooms and personal possessions, and against coercion in seeking admission of guilt in infractions of rules. The ordinary requirements for lawful search are normally to be followed.

A student involved in an infraction should be assured by the board's delegated disciplinary officer that he has the privilege of a hearing before a regularly constituted hearing committee. The hearing procedure follows proper legal procedures including testimony, witness, cross-examination, defense, record of hearing, and right of appeal. The student should be notified in writing of his offense, and of the time of hearing. He should be granted sufficient time to prepare his defense.

The disciplinary procedure must have a valid legal foundation, because this is an area in which the college can be sued.

A recent California court decision in a case stemming from the so-called "filthy speech movement" at the University of California's Berkeley campus in 1965 may become the leading case on the authority of colleges and universities regarding student discipline. Information on the case was recently compiled by John Caffre, director of the Council's Commission Administrative Affairs.

In March 1965 four students in good standing on the Berkeley campus sparked and led the so-called "filthy speech movement." This involved public readings from novels, and a "cheer" which consisted of spelling out and the uttering an Anglo-Saxon four-letter obscenity. After hearings and proceedings, complicated by the arrest of three of the students, one student was dismissed and three were suspended from the university. The four students sued the university for reinstatement, contending violation of free speech, "unconstitutionally vague and overbroad" regulation, and denial of due process. The trial court sustained the university, the students appealed, and on February 28, 1967, the Court of Appeal unanimously affirmed the judgment. On April 26 the California Supreme

Court, unanimously and without opinion, denied further hearing. The case has been final since that date.

Considered on the most significant findings of the court is the following: "We hold that in this case, the university's disciplinary action was a proper exercise of its inherent general powers to maintain order on the campus and to exclude therefrom those who are detrimental to its well-being. . . . Thus . . . it is necessary to discuss plaintiffs' contention that any particular regulation was unconstitutionally vague." Following are other highlights from the decision in the case, *Goldberg v. Regents of the University of California*:

°The regents have the general rule-making or policy-making power in regard to the university . . . and are [with exceptions not material here] fully empowered with respect to the organization and government of the university . . . including the authority to maintain order and decorum on the campus and the enforcement of same by all appropriate means . . .

°The more recent Federal cases stress the importance of education to the individual and conclude that attendance in a state university is no longer considered a privilege . . . but is now regarded as an important benefit.

°For constitutional purposes, the better approach . . . recognizes that state universities should no longer stand in *loco parentis* in relation to their students.

°Rather, attendance at publicly financed institutions of higher education should be regarded as a benefit somewhat analogous to that of public employment. . . . The test is whether conditions annexed to the benefit reasonably tend to further the purposes sought by conferment of that benefit and whether the utility of imposing the conditions manifestly outweights any resulting impairment of constitutional rights.

°[The students'] argument has as its major unarticulated premise that since their purpose was to protest, they had a constitutional right to do so whenever, however, and wherever they pleased. That concept of constitutional law was vigorously and forthrightly rejected by the United States Supreme Court. . . .

°Thus, the university has the power to formulate and enforce rules of student conduct that are appropriate and necessary to the maintenance of order and propriety, considering the accepted norms of social behavior in the community, where such rules are reasonably necessary to further the university's educational goals.

°Historically, the academic community has been unique in having its own standards, rewards, and punishment. . . . Thus, in an academic community, greater freedoms and greater restrictions may prevail than in society at large, and the subtle fixing of these limits should, in large measure, be left to the educational institution itself.

°The association with an educational institution as a student requires certain minimum standards of propriety in conduct. . . . Conduct involving rowdiness, rioting, the destruction of property, the reckless display of impropriety or any unjustifiable disturbance of the public order on or off campus is indefensible whether it is incident to an athletic event, the advent of spring, or the devotion, however sincere, to some cause or ideal.

°[A leading case has noted that procedures for dismissing college students were not analogous to criminal proceedings and could not be so without being both impractical and detrimental to the educational atmosphere and functions of a university. . . . The court noted that where the student misconduct (as opposed to failure to meet academic standards) depended on a collection of facts easily colored by the point of view of various witnesses (as here), there should be a hearing with an opportunity to hear both sides. However, it was made clear that a full-dress judicial hearing, with the right to cross-examine witnesses, was not required, as such a hearing, with the attending publicity and disturbance of university activities, might be detrimental to the educational atmosphere of the university and impractical to carry out.]

°While recognizing that the disciplinary measures that were imposed may have a very serious effect upon the careers of the individual plaintiffs, the disciplinary measures . . . amounted to a denial of a benefit and can by no stretch of the imagination be classified as criminal proceedings.

°[The] university, as an academic community, can formulate its own standards, rewards, and punishments to achieve its educational objectives. . . . Thus, except for the applicable constitutional limitations, the relationship between appropriate university rules and laws of the outside community is entirely coincidental.

°[The university's] committee was operating properly within constitutional limitations. Its recognition of the interest of the academic community in resolving its disciplinary matters swiftly does not invade any area occupied by [California] state law.

°We conclude . . . that plaintiffs' complaint does not state a cause of action on any theory.[5]

Student Publications

The college trustee picks up the student newspaper and scans it quickly to see if any outrageous article is included in this particular issue, breathes a sigh of relief, and settles down to read more leisurely an article about Saturday's football game or a review of a recent lecture by a government official.

Most college trustees have an uneasy, nervous attitude toward student publications. And why not? Colleges have been stung often by student publications. Several cases could be cited. We will mention two. In 1962 the student newspaper at the University of Colorado published an essay which violently denounced Senator Barry Goldwater. When the

[5] *Higher Education and National Affairs,* "California Court Decision Expected To Be Leading Case on Student Discipline," Vol. XVI, No. 34 (Oct. 6, 1967), p. 4–5.

[6] Orley R. Herron and Edward E. Ericson, "How To Organize Control of Your Student Publications," *College and University Business,* Vol. 43, No. 4 (Oct. 1967), pp. 4–10.

case came before the university's Board of Publications, the student editor was told that he had been guilty of printing libel, but the Board made no move to fire him. However, the president of the university overrode the position of the Board of Publications and dismissed the student editor. Then in 1967 the two student editors of the yearbook at Grinnell College attempting to produce a unique work—to depict campus life as they felt it really was. When the printer received the copy, he sent it back to the college and said that he would not print it unless he was absolved of any libel suits that might result. The college authorities sought legal counsel and were advised that the book contained about thirty libelous pictures, which would have to be removed before the yearbook could be safely printed. However the student editors refused to remove the crucial pictures. Thus the administration decided to scrap the yearbook altogether for that year.

The uneasiness of trustees over student publications is based on a healthy respect for the power of the printed and pictorial page. It is also based on an accurate concept of modern students as more assertive and more articulate and at the same time more iconoclastic and more suspect toward traditional values than ever before. Recognizing the currency of this problem, what should be the trustee's attitude toward student publications?

First, there must be an understanding of the nature of student publications. What is their purpose? Why do they exist? Also, there must be some clear guidelines governing the posture which trustees take toward the publications.

Doubtless some of the queasiness which trustees feel toward student publications is based on a faulty understanding of what the publications should be doing. Let us state some general principles.

1. Student publications are not public relations pieces. They are not written to present the picture of the school which the administration holds or wants presented to the public.

2. Student newspapers are not merely a calendar or chronicle of activities on the campus. They should not be limited to straight news reporting—no more than a city newspaper is so limited.

3. Student publications are the vehicles for the representation of the student mind. This must include experimentation with the expression of new and original ideas.

4. By-lined columns are to be read as the opinion of the writer only, not as representing the opinions of the staff of the paper or the position of the school.

5. The test for the inclusion of a piece in a literary publication is that of artistic integrity, not morality or adherence to traditional values.

6. If the student publication has a faculty advisor—and most still do—the trustee must understand that the advisor is no more than an advisor. He does not make the final decision on the publication, nor is he a censor; he only recommends.

7. Final responsibility for what is published must obviously be vested somewhere. It must be clear where this authority lies.

8. Since these publications are directly controlled by students, the selection of student editors is the key to smooth handling of this whole matter. Once a poor choice has been made, there is little that can be done.

9. The goal in a student publication is a representative sampling of student thinking. Student publications are not channels for the constant iteration of a viewpoint that is radical in relation to the thinking of the student body as a whole.

10. Efforts at direct control or censorship of student publications by administrators deal only with the results of the problem, not with the cause. Furthermore, the radical opinions will find ways of getting circulated on the campus—the latest being through the spate of antiestablishment publications appearing on the fringes of many large university campuses. No matter how well a student publication succeeds in presenting a balanced view of the mood of the campus, there will always be some who feel they are underrepresented. Indeed, some want not a balanced view at all, but rather a mouthpiece for propaganda; and if they cannot make a mouthpiece of the school publications, they will resort to the underground approach.

Now that we have listed some of the principles which must be understood as the trustee confronts student publications, let us proceed to a list of recommendations delineating what is the judicious stance for trustees to assume. As the author fully recognizes, certain campuses have unique situations that will not be covered by these suggestions. The recommendations should be considered general guidelines for a school which desires to take a moderate approach to the matter of student publications.

1. Anticipate problems by establishing the proper machinery for handling them. The next two recommendations give details of the suggested machinery.

2. Establish a Student Affairs Committee on the Board of Trustees. With all of the current talk of the "generation gap," it is incumbent on adults who are charged with the education of the young to show genuine interest in their special problems and needs. Important as buildings are to the contemporary educational scene, students are even more important. Trustees should pay at least as much attention to students as to build-

ings. And though some teachers might not be pleased to admit it, it seems obvious that students have greater influence on students than teachers have.

3. Establish a Publications Board to exercise final responsibility for all student publications. An organizational chart follows:

The composition of the Publications Board is debatable; it is also crucial. One view would be to have a majority of faculty and administration and a minority of students. The major drawback to this arrangement is that the final authority for what students are allowed to express resides with those who are not students. Another view would be to have students only. The major drawback in this case is their lack of experience and maturity when faced with sometimes difficult decisions. The author's recommendation is that the board have a majority of students with a minority of administrators and faculty members. Then the final decision on what is printed by students is not taken out of the hands of the students. At the same time, the students are not deprived of the counsel and experience of veterans of the academic community. College is supposed to provide a learning situation. The composition of the Publications Board which is recommended is the one best suited to accomplish this goal.

4. Do not allow the established machinery to be bypassed. If a trustee has a complaint against something appearing in a student publication, he should take it to the Publications Board via an administrator, probably the president. In no case should there be a direct confrontation between a trustee and a student editor or faculty advisor.

5. Do not interrupt the circulation of a specific issue of a student publication except on legal counsel—that is, if a legal consultant advises that the issue contains libel or obscenity. It is desirable, of course, that student publications reflect good taste, but it is up to the student editors (with counsel from faculty advisors) to determine whether the canons of good taste are violated.

6. Give the student body some credit for discrimination in their receiving of ideas. As any regular reader of a letters-to-the-editor column of a college newspaper knows, college students do not just absorb unthinkingly what other students have to say. The chances are good that a radical article will be replied to and taken care of by other students, as long as administrators and trustees do not interfere. Of course, it is possible that what strikes trustees as radical ideas will not seem so to the student generation, in which case trustees must simply recognize and allow for values other than their own. The key matter in this recommendation is to allow ideas to compete in the open market place of intellectual activity.

7. See to it that a sound screening process is devised for the selection of student editors. The following steps are recommended:

(a) The decision should be made by the Publications Board.

(b) The application process should insist on a letter which states the applicant's philosophy toward the position sought and also the goals which he sets for his tenure in that position.

(c) The Publications Board should seek the recommendations and counsel of previous editors, faculty advisors, and any other persons who they feel have knowledge relevant to the selection of the new editor.

(d) The selection should be made on the basis of the suitability of the applicant for the position; there should be no extraneous criteria. Of course, this is not to negate the need for selecting someone who agrees with the philosophy that student publications should be representative of the thinking of the whole student body and not just of his own, but that is itself one element in determining the applicant's suitability for the position. We cannot overemphasize the importance of this step of selection of the student editors. Once the student editor is chosen, the die is cast. If the choice turns out to have been an unfortunate one, the best thing to do is to try to endure the year (or whatever the tenure may be). If the situation becomes intolerable, then the proper machinery for removal of a student editor (through Publications Board, etc.,) must be used, but this cannot be done without placing great strain on the fabric of the campus community.

8. Faculty advisors should see copy before it reaches print. Otherwise, there is no opportunity for them to do their advising, and the reason

for being in the position of faculty advisor ceases to exist. This may seem obvious and elementary, but it is possible that this procedure is not regularly followed in a majority of cases. If the faculty advisor is a titular and not functional position, then the learning experience for the editorial staff and through them for the whole student body is thwarted. When the faculty advisor informs the student editor that he is available if needed, ·he asks the students to take the initiative in their getting together. Not only is this inconvenient, but some student editors would feel that calling for help was an admission of lack of independence and maturity, and others would cockily trust their own judgment when they should not.

9. Because of the practical difficulty of putting out a daily paper, we recommend that dailies have more than one faculty advisor so that the task of advising can be done properly.

10. Student publications should have stated advertising policy. There are federal statutes regulating advertising, and the governing boards should be advised regarding them. There is a high rate of turnover in student editorial positions, because the jobs are so demanding that most student editors find it difficult to maintain quality performance in their academic work. Because of this, as many guidelines and aids as possible should be available to the new editors in order to insure the desired continuity in the publication. Advertising can be a very sensitive area, and it should not be ignored as an unimportant one.

There is a danger that governing boards will be too permissive in dealing with the sensitive subject of student publications. In particular, some boards will shy away from involving themselves at all in this area because of the fear of charges of restriction and invasion of academic freedom. But if this area is as important in the total program of the college as the author believes, the board will be shirking its responsibility if it pays no attention to the problems that can arise from student publications.

But if there is a danger of overpermissiveness, the danger of restrictiveness is probably even greater, especially since teachers and students are highly sensitive to any infringement in this direction. Involvement is not equivalent to usurpation. Proper trustee involvement requires the recognition of the nature of student publications—that they are *student* publications. In the final analysis, a college cannot safeguard itself from its students.

SUMMARY

The most important single factor in the direction of higher education is the board of trustees. It is the college board which selects the administration, assembles a faculty, and in a myriad of ways shapes the campus both physically and philosophically. At the typical American college it is the governing board that directs both present day progress and the long-range destiny of the institution. This mandate becomes remarkably complex. The college governing body wrestles with the building codes, housing arrangements, wills and bequests, and the strategies of fund-raising, student affairs, and budget construction. Above all, the board must see to it that all subordinate functions mix in a way that ultimately meets the institution's educational needs. The board deals mainly in three areas: (1) policy formation, (2) selecting long-range objectives, (3) long-range strategic planning. The bylaws and statutes set forth the boundaries of the board prerogatives. The ends and means of the implementation of the directional boundaries are evidenced in the pattern of delegation and advisement. The nature of student affairs requires a thorough understanding of its variegated vectors if the board is to guide an institution ably.

QUESTIONS

1. What are the general powers of the board relative to their duties?
2. Why is the board of trustees the most important single factor in the direction of higher education?
3. Describe the style of management that should be the nature of the board in budget analysis.
4. Where should the abilities and talents of the board be centered upon within the control of an institution?
5. What role is the best for the board to assume relative to academic governance?
6. Analyze the nature of student publications and the board position on them.

BIBLIOGRAPHY

BECK, HUBERT P. *Men Who Control Our Universities*, New York: Kings Crown Press, 1947.

BLACKWELL, T. E. *College Law: A Guide for Administrators*, Washington, D.C.: American Council on Education 1961.

BURGESS, KENNETH F. "The Trustees' Function in Today's Universities and Colleges," *Association of American Colleges. Bulletin*, XLIV (October 1959), pp. 396–407.

CAPEN, SAMUEL P. *The Management of Universities*, Buffalo, New York: Foster and Stewart Publishing Company, 1953, XII.

CARMICHAEL, J. P. "Public Trusteeship: Pegasus or Dead Horse," *Association of Governing Board Proceedings* (1956), pp. 38–48.

CORSON, JOHN J. *Goverance of Colleges and Universities*. New York: McGraw-Hill, 1960.

COWLEY, WILLIAM H. "The Administration of American Colleges and Universities," O. Nelson, *University Administration in Practice*, Palo Alto: Stanford University Press, 1958.

DIBDEN, A. J. "Role of Administrators and Trustees: A Faculty View," *Association of American College Bulletin*, XLIV (December 1958), pp. 536–544.

DEUTCH, MONROE E. *The College From Within*. Berkeley, Calif.: U. of California Press, 1952.

DICKHOFF, JOHN S. *Tomorrow's Professors*. New York: Fund for the Advancement of Education, 1959.

EELLS, WALTER C. "Boards of Control of Universities and Colleges," *The Educational Record*, XLII (October 1961), pp. 336–342.

ELIOT, CHARLES W. *University Administration*. Boston, Mass.: Houghton Mifflin, 1908.

ELLIOT, EDWARD L., M. M. CHAMBERS, and WILLIAM A. ASHBROOK. *The Government of Higher Education*. New York: American Book, 1935.

HEALD, HENRY T. "A Trustee's Responsibilities," in Proceedings Association of Boards of State Universities and Allied Institutions (1954), pp. 62–67.

HENDERSON, ALGO D. *Policies and Practices in Higher Education*, New York: Harper, 1960.

HETZEL, R. "What Are the Central Responsibilities of the Trustees Which Apply Both to Publicly and to Privately Supported Institutions?," in *Current Issues in Higher Education*, Washington, D.C., Association for Higher Education, 1960, pp. 153–156.

HUGHES, RAYMOND M. *A Manual for Trustees of Colleges and Universities*. Ames, Iowa: Iowa State College Press, 1943.

MARTORANA, S. V., and ERNEST V. HOLLIS. *State Boards Responsible for Higher Education*, U.S. Office of Education, Circular No. 619, Washington, D.C.: Government Printing Office, 1960.

McBRIDE, K. "The Role of Trustees," *Journal of Higher Education*, (November 1959), pp. 432–434.

PRESTHUS, R. V. "Authority in Organization," in S. Marlick and E. Van Ness, *Concepts and Issues in Administrative Behavior*. Englewood Cliffs, N.J.: Prentice-Hall, 1962.

RANK, MORTON. *College and University Trusteeship*. Yellow Springs, Ohio: Antioch Press, 1959.

RUSSELL, JOHN DALE. "Changing Pattern of Administration in Higher Education," Annals of The American Academy of Political and Social Science, CCCI (September 1955), pp. 22–31.

TAYLOR, HAROLD. *On Education and Freedom*. New York: Abelard-Schuman, 1954.

TEAD, ORDWAY. *Administration: Its Purpose and Performance*, New York: Harper and Brothers, 1959.

————. "College Trustees, Their Opportunities and Duties," *Journal of Higher Education*, XXII (April 1951), pp. 171–180.

"The Role of the College and University Trustees," Summary of a discussion by the trustees of the Carnegie Foundation for the Advancement of Teaching, Reprinted from the 1961–62 Annual Report.

CHAPTER 3

The President

THE PRESIDENT AND THE BOARD OF TRUSTEES

The history of the office of president in American colleges and universities began with the election of Mr. Henry Bunster as chief officer of Harvard College in 1640. He received the title of president, which has since become the usual title for the chief executive of American institutions of higher learning. Three other terms have been used to identify the executive board: rector, chancellor, and provost.

The history of the presidency also reveals that nine-tenths of the college presidents who served before the Civil War were ordained ministers. Schmidt found that with the exception of President John Leverett of Harvard (1708–24) not a single lay president was appointed during the entire Colonial period.[1]

During the early years prior to the Civil War, 182 colleges were founded and survived, but during the Civil War 400 new institutions opened and all failed. Since most of the presidents were ministers, the presidents returned to the pulpit following the closing of their school.

After the Civil War, however, the trend to elect men apart from the clergy as president of colleges and universities became common. The trend has continued so that most college presidents are selected from the ranks of higher education. Stephens cited that, "contrary to popular belief, the proportion of presidents selected from occupations outside higher education does not seem to have increased materially since 1900"[2] He also detected that whereas the presidents of the larger institutions tend to have studied the social sciences, presidents of smaller colleges or universities are most likely to have studied education or theology.[3]

In consideration of a president, a board of trustees may expect to seek a new president every eight years. The years of service of college presidents range from 5.8 for Catholic institutions to 9.7 years for presidents

[1] Ralph Praetor, *The College President* (Washington, D.C., 1963) p. 3.
[2] E. V. Stanford, "Functional Board of Trustees for the Catholic College," *Catholic Education Review,* LIX, p. 85.
[3] *Ibid.,* p. 90.

42

in both public and private colleges. In regard to academic degrees, over 60 percent of university and college presidents serving today have earned doctorates.

As one reviews the history of the office of the college president, it is quite apparent that the selection of the person for this office is one of the supreme tasks of the board of trustees. Ralph Praetor remarked that "the selection of a president for an institution of higher education is one of the most, if not the most important duties of a board of trustees."[4] It is important because the president automatically becomes the chief liaison between the board and the institution. The manner in which he executes his responsibility can and will set the tone of the academic enterprise.

The board must be reminded that the role of the president is complex and multifaceted and needs clear definition before selection of a candidate for that role can be finalized. The board of trustees should define the task of the president in light of the needs, objectives, and philosophy of their institution. The board should also realize that a successful president of one institution does not automatically insure that he will be a successful president in another. The selection of a president must be carefully thought out and his appointment should only be made after every avenue and resource has been exhausted. A mistake in the appointment to his office can prove to be very costly.

Harold Stoke, in *The American College President*, stated regarding the selection of a college presidency: "One thing is clear: colleges must have presidents and it makes a great deal of difference who they are."[5]

The relationship of the president to the board of trustees is an extremely crucial one. The president can establish a smooth line of communication or build imaginary barriers that create havoc in the academic confines. He is the chief representative of all avenues of the institution to the board of trustees, and this is a responsibility that cannot be delegated. The president must take full responsibility for the operation of affairs of a growing complex of higher learning. Praetor has stated that:

> In working with the board of trustees the president is ever conscious of his responsibility to assist them to understand and appreciate the educational program and the needs of the institution. He is responsible for the two-way communication between the campus communities and the board, and in the process he needs to emphasize the special responsibilities expected of the agencies whose activities he correlates . . . Therefore the president has to be a skillfull blender of different points of view which will result in decisions being respected by all agencies affected.[6]

[4] Praetor, *op. cit.*, p. 58.
[5] Harold W. Stoke, *The American College President* (New York: Harper, 1959), p. 20.
[6] Praetor, *op. cit.*, pp. 58–59.

One of the first tasks of the president should be the reviewing of the structure of the board of trustees and suggest ways of structuring the board so that trustees become involved to the maximum degree. Trustees need to be involved, and the president can direct their involvement in a variety of ways. The president must also realize that the academic community has entrusted to him the professional hopes and aspirations they want to actualize at the institution. If the president is not willing to shoulder the mantle of responsibility, he should step aside and let those equal to the task carry on.

History has shown that the combination of an inadequate president and an indecisive board can spell the doom for an institution, whereas a top chief executive officer can motivate the academic enterprise and a potentially good board to heights previously unattained.

The president, by virtue of his office, is the major decision maker apart from the board of trustees. Though the president's role is multifarious and his work is multilateral, his opportunities for influence in decision making are very broad. He is the power center for decisions and he must be careful how he exerts that power.

Harold Stoke remarked regarding this power:

> . . . Those who enjoy it are not very successful and those who are successful are not very happy. The explanation is hidden somewhere in the philosophy of power. Those who enjoy exercising the power shouldn't have it and those who should exercise it are not likely to enjoy it.[7]

In arriving at decisions, the president has the responsibility of choosing the particular course of action and direction deemed best from the alternatives of all the communities represented. The ability to make those decisions and implement them assumes a trust vested in him by not only the trustees but by the faculty, staff, students, and public as well. This trust given to him by his associates will either grow or decline, based upon his method of operation in daily decision making throughout the year. His ability to get things accomplished may depend to a great extent on that trust. Remember, people are led only to the degree that they want to be led. The president must inspire his associates to follow him as their leader or the institution will be steered on a shaky course.

One of the major roles of the president will be to submit information to the board concerning the total college program. Any presentation made by the president to the board of trustees must be based on sound, reasonable, and rational foundations. The facts presented must merit their consideration at the board level, and controversial items must not be hidden because of fear of board reprisal. In my research regarding boards, I discovered that presidents have a tendency to shield board members from information that would cause dissatisfaction to the board.

[7] Stoke, *loc. cit.*

Trustee members need to know the truth if they are to make the most adequate decisions necessary for the ongoing of an institution. If they cannot accept the responsibility of knowing these verities, they are not fulfilling their calling.

The nature of the role of the president and the role of the trustees demands that they operate in an environment that brings cohesive union concerning the major vectors of the institution. This does not imply that the two must agree in all areas touching their responsibility. It simply means that the president and the board, for the well-being of the institution, must be able to negotiate, facilitate, develop, and lead on a priority level of good communication one with the other. The problems of growth, by necessity, involve tension, difficulty, and stress, yet they do not require division, disunity, and disrespect to prevail.

The president is charged with the responsibility of maintaining proper and appropriate relations with the board. Not, however, at the expense or diversion of the college program.

If there is a poor working relationship between the board and the president it cannot be hidden. If it is not resolved, it will soon destroy the academic morale of an institution, no matter how prestigious that institution might be.

I submit that the beginning of a great institution is the selection of a strong, flexible board of trustees who will appoint a top-level chief executive. If that chief executive is willing to do the job that has to be done within the entire academic enterprise—which involves maintaining the proper role with all communities of the institution, including his relationship with the board of trustees—the future of education is greatly enhanced.[8]

Henry Wreston wrote that:

> Managing to live with a board of trustees is like riding a spirited horse that is very skittish. Trustees will shy at the shadow rather more quickly than at real danger. Nevertheless, people like to ride spirited horses and after one has learned that art it is a thrilling experience and never boring.[9]

Make sure the right jockey is on that spirited horse!

GUIDELINES FOR GOVERNING BOARDS AND COLLEGE PRESIDENTS

The recent study of college presidents, headed by James Perkins, Cornell University President, attracts new attention upon the role of the

[8] Orley R. Herron, "Crucial Test for Trustees: Selecting College President," *College and University Business Journal*, Vol. 43, No. 2 (August 1967), pp. 8–12.
[9] Henry M. Wreston, *Academic Processions, Reflections of a College President* (New York: Columbia U.P., 1959), p. 116.

president as a leader of the academic enterprise. The office of the president ought to be reviewed, because each year about 250 new college presidents are selected to fill the vacancies in higher education. It is imperative, therefore, that reflections of the presidency and governing boards be critically examined.

The board of trustees' most important function is to select a president. No other matter has greater implication or significance than that selection. The president can either make or break an institution. Before a board can select a president it must define his role in light of the institution's objectives and must understand how that role conforms to the total spectrum of higher education. In the selection of a president, a board must remember that the role involves interaction with many varied and diversified types of people. A president who does not understand people or is not willing to interact with people is not destined long for the presidency. Many of the president's problems are "people" problems; he must be a connoisseur of individuals. Presidents who don't have the tact of a diplomat and the negotiating art of a statesman are in for trouble. The board has three guidelines to consider in their relationship with the president.

1. No one shall be hired within an institution without the recommendation of the president.

2. The president makes the budget and recommends it to the board.

3. The president must be elected unanimously.

No one should be hired within an institution without the president's recommendation. The board can recommend or suggest good employees to a president but must never let the board hire a faculty member, administrator, or a staff member without the president's recommendation. To do so is to undermine his authority, weaken his prerogative, and strain his image within the institution. The president must have the responsibility and authority to recommend all employees for the institution. He is the elected agent of the board and will only recommend someone to be hired that is qualified within the framework of their educational commitment. The president has the machinery in staff to secure the best candidates for their institution. The department heads and other faculty members know their own particular requirements and recommend to the president the individuals competent to meet these necessities. Boards that choose to interfere with the hiring of staff usurp the prerogative of the president and will not have a strong academic institution. Boards are not trained to hire faculty and staff and have little understanding of the specific prerequisites and qualifications for these positions. The board members, though highly professional in every sense, are amateurs in the analysis of specific needs, both academically and staffwise. The board must leave the hiring to the delegated authorities and react and respond to the president's recommendations.

The president makes the budget and recommends it to the board. The budget is the president's prerogative to develop. The board's prerogative is to analyze, review, and approve it. The internal machinery allocates the budget within the institutions. Most college budgets are multimillion-dollar documents and are quite extensive. The board should concern itself with the major items of the budget and not scrutinize its minute details. The board can expect a budget that is most ideal if they permit the president to have authority in all phases of its construction. A wise president will permit faculty and administrative staff to participate in the development of the budget. In this respect a consensus can be arrived at which permits greater morale, better understanding, and fuller commitment to the goals of that budget. Budgets are usually too enormous to allow haphazard construction, poor accounting, and improper allocation. The president is obligated to set up an adequate organization to handle the technicalities of the budget. Poor stewardship and guardianship in budgeting should not occur in an institution of higher education which must have lofty ideals of integrity. Boards that choose to handle all picayune details of the budget and spend laborious hours "nit-picking" will evolve "small boards" philosophically. Higher education does not need any more additions to this already too large grouping. As a board, permit the president to effect the budget and then be pliant to it.

The president must be elected unanimously. A board should never permit a president to consent to join their institution who is not elected unanimously. No president should assume his office without the unanimous vote of confidence by the board. Even with support, the role of the president is difficult enough; without the full support of the board, the job is practically impossible to carry out. Consensus is the key to smooth operation in an institution of higher learning, and the board must demand it, but with a unanimous endorsement in the selection of the president. Presidents are only human and to assume this office with the knowledge that they are a compromise candidate with a divided vote is asking too much. It is better for the board to wait the extra time to have a unanimous selection than to hire a president with a split vote. There are few guarantees to success in academic administration; a unanimous vote is one of the guarantees of a good foundation for strong administration.

TIME

No president ever has enough time to do the job he is selected to execute. The role of the president requires involvement in a myriad of activities which are physically and emotionally exhausting. There are many special events that he should attend and many people whom it is incumbent on him to receive. The president must be a careful budgeter of his time or the rat race will engulf him. He is obligated to decide what things he can do and what things he can delegate to others. The role is often so multifaceted that the president's mind can be like a checker-board with all the moves plotted in advance; he may become so fretful he cannot give his best individual attention to anything. The president cannot be omniscient or omnipresent; those that try to be become nerv-ous wrecks. A wise president will select a staff who can assist him in the most appropriate and adequate disbursement of his time. They will guard the president from being trapped by subjective personal prefer-ence and help him to remain philosophically objective as their com-mander-in-chief. The open-door policy is the best, but it cannot become a revolving door which keeps the president always in the state of motion. The president must provide for a proper balance of his time so there is a mixture of work and play. The trustees must be ever cognizant of the president's mental welfare and encourage him to relax while making ef-forts to relieve him of some of the anxieties of his job.

Presidents who become physically or emotionally spent day after day will not be the most articulate or the sharpest leaders. The mind and body should be strong or the pressures that exist will never be eradi-cated. The president and his allocation of time are essential to the success of the institution.

ENVIRONMENT

The president and the board are responsible in a great measure for what type of environment evolves upon their campus. The atmosphere created, whether it be a codal environment or a loosely structured pos-ture, sets the tone of the enterprise. The rigidity or flexibility of the trustees, a friendly or depersonalized campus social strata, an authori-tarian or democratic attitude of administrative control, a heterogeneous, homogeneous, demographic representation, a cosmopolitan or provincial structure—all these are vectors contributing to the maturation of the environment. The president and board make a great deal of difference in the type of atmosphere that will be either perpetuated or abolished on their campus. The president, more than any other individual, sets the tone of the academic community. Tradition plays a major role in the transmission of values and attitudes from one campus generation to the next. The president must be constantly aware of the climate that per-vades his campus, and must strive for the optimum climate in all areas. If the campus environment is not what it should be, the president is obligated to oil the machinery so as to elicit the necessary changes. Major changes in the environment structure do not come easily, and the president must not be discouraged when his timetable for change is torn asunder. Norms, regulations, people, events, styles of interaction, policies, class structure, financial security, priorities of interest, identification and construction on issues are all embedded in the generating of the climate control for the campus. The channels of communication must be open to the president so that he may know the temperature of its environment. Unnecessary onslaught can overtake a campus if the president is not "tuned in" on the daily atmosphere of the institution. Every campus has a direct personality which must be constantly reexamined, reworked, and upgraded for the best interests of the institution and its purposes in society.

PERSONAL RELATIONS

Personal relations are high on the priority of essentials in the presidential role. The president, no matter how hard he tries, can never escape people. The manner in which he displays courtesy, tact, diplomacy, friendship, and firmness may mean the difference between a smooth or bumpy administrative process. The president sets the example in person-to-person interactions and confrontations. He is the topic of conversations, coffee breaks, back-door gossip, sessions, seminars, and a bushel of other communication styles. The president, on the one hand, must maintain a respectful distance; yet on the other hand, he must reveal a warmth and genuine concern for all. His own personality and bias will automatically attract him to certain people, but he must guard against preferential treatment or prejudicial arbitration. People are his business and he must stand strong in the analysis of human understanding. Inconsiderate or ill-advised displays of personal relationships can create isolation spots or credibility gaps between the president and certain groups in the academic community. Favoritism must never invade his domain, and if it does the critics will not be merciful. The president is obligated to understand and know the varigated groupings on his campus. He should organize his staff in such a way that he has access and knowledge, coupled with understanding, as to what are the concerns of the people; he should be adept at administering. Each board member should be invited regularly to the president's home for dinner so that they can view each other socially as well as professionally. Every effort should be made to understand the board. If the president is to be their agent, their liaison, their leader, then he must know of whom he speaks. Many a trustee has said he has never been invited to dine in the president's home. The trustees in turn should strive to know the president apart from his office and this understanding may be the tonic for vigorous leadership in the future. Lack of understanding of people is excusable if the president tries to learn about his command; it is his irresponsibility if he is not willing to learn.

GLASS HOUSES

University and college presidents live in glass houses. This is not good but it is one of the hazards of the presidential occupation. The president's moves are not very secret and a chronicle of his "activities" is constantly under surveillance. Nor are members of his family free from daily observation, and many a president has returned to the security of the professorial role to escape the "glass house" philosophy. The president and particularly his wife are in demand for attendance at the regularly scheduled events on campus, many of which occur on the same night. He holds teas, dinners, and discussions in his home so that in some sense he becomes community property. There are few ways to escape the glass house; the president must learn to live with it. But at least he can understand why the "glass house" atmosphere pervades his domain. He is the symbol of so many ideas, policies, and events within the institution, and no one can really take his place. The president is in constant demand and his every move is becoming more programmed so that he may more fully serve the vested interests of the consensus. The president and his family must capitalize on the rare "quiet time" of privacy that they may occasionally enjoy, and must learn to give understanding to one another. The family life can complement and harmonize with the presidential duties if it is a total family project. Although extra effort and sacrifice may be essential to counteract the "glass house," it nevertheless can be fun and extremely rewarding.

PUBLIC-PRIVATE

There are many public and many private institutions of higher learning. Regarding the presidency, there are many similarities between the office of the president of a public institution and that of a private one. There are however, various differences. Some public institutions have strong political influences and overtones. If this is the case, then the president must understand sophistically the legislative and political process. The president, in a real sense, must develop a politician's thick skin so as not to be sensitive to the overwhelming political pressures that confront him. Political pressures are manifold depending upon the nature of environment of the state and even the nation. The Joe McCarthy era, the loyalty oath proceedings, the beatniks, the civil rights issues, the war concerns all may affect the philosophical foundations of administrative control. Some state institutions have much stronger political influences than others. Political pressures are not an easy situation for any executive, and particularly for the chief executive of an academic institution. The wise president will learn to interact appropriately to the political pressures and will not be swept under by the waves. Political pressures have a tendency to blow hot and cold, high and low, depending upon the political climate of the state. Election years for governships can produce the greatest debates of politics and education than any other. Many a governor is turning to higher education and making it a campaign issue of an election. The president will be discreet in showing political favoritism regarding the governor's race during election years. He should stay out of recommending publicly or supporting openly a particular candidate. That is not his task and it is precarious ground to enter.

PRESIDENTIAL TRANSMISSION

New presidents will be selected about every eight years. A board member, therefore, may select three or four presidents during his service as a trustee. Some presidents are going to do a better job than others. Good predecessors have a way of overshadowing new presidents. A board and faculty can be critical appraisers of comparison and can make it quite difficult for a new president. A positive, orderly process should occur in presidential succession. Former presidents are to be reverenced, reviewed, and analyzed; however, such attitudes in themselves cannot run the institution once they have left it. Some trustees and faculty become so dependent and idolatrous about a former president that it would take a "superhuman" president to dispel this fantasy image. A board must establish an adequate machinery to handle the transition from one president to another. A new president must be given adequate support, confidence, and authority to take over the reins of the institution. If a former president had a difficult and tempestuous time with the board, the faculty, or alumni, the board must exert considerable effort to provide an open atmosphere for the new successor. This is why the president must be elected unanimously so that he is not under a cloud even before he begins. The board is obligated to review with the president all information pertinent and necessary for his initiation. The board should not hide bad information that the new president needs to know to make a candid appraisal of the situation he faces. The board is obligated to strengthen the staff of the president and not handicap or hinder it through improper or inadequate information disclosures. On the other hand, the board should guard against exaggeration or underestimation. The new president is looking for everything he can find to do the best job he can. The style the board employs in presidential succession is a key to that success.

SELECTION

Selecting a president is a task of the board and one that should be given its most scrupulous attention. The selection process is tantamount to obtaining the most capable person for the job. The board can follow some guidelines to ensure an orderly process in the selection. Having formulated the goals of the institution, the board must now formulate the job description and expectation of the new president. It must know what type of individual it is seeking before it begins the process of interviews. An extremely useful step is to establish a committee of the board that is empowered to search the program candidates for consideration.

The faculty may have a committee which can advise the board on their desires. The board committee can serve as a screening committee and recommend to the full board eligible candidates for consideration. The interview process should involve detailed investigation of the background, education, and experience of potential candidates. Success in job experience is a prerequisite to consideration.

An individual who has been successful at a previous institution is more likely to be a success at your institution. People who have created ill-will, and have been highly unsatisfactory at other institutions should be carefully examined in or before the interview, but they should not be automatically eliminated, merely because their former job experience was unsatisfactory—the environment may have not been conducive to bringing out their finest capabilities.

The board should not neglect their own campus in its search for a president. The ideal president may already be working on your campus so do not automatically eliminate the home-grown candidate, although some boards choose to do so. Take time to interview and explore potential candidates. Hasty decisions are costly and must be avoided. It is wise to invite the wife of a candidate to visit the campus while her husband is being reviewed. The wife is an important person in the life of the president and should be a complement rather than a detriment to his work. A person with a background in education is more qualified than those outside the field for a presidency. The academic enterprise is a curious species and needs one of its own to understand it. There have been notable exceptions to this and the board will have to make its own decision once it has weighed the evidence.

THE PRESIDENT AND FRINGE BENEFITS

There are some benefits that a board should consider as norms for the president. The first is that his salary is to be set by the board and should be a reasonable compensation. No one in the institution should be paid more than the president. The board must realize that the president is the chief executive of a multimillion-dollar operation. If he were to be president of a 30- or 50-million dollar enterprise in business, he would receive a very commensurate salary.

It is mandatory that the board constantly review the president's salary. A committee of the board could survey other institutions of comparable size, assets, or philosophy and analyze the presidential office to determine if the president's salary is in line with these others.

The president's salary sets the ceiling on the other salaries within the institution. The board should be generous in the salary commitments to the president. His job is literally a twenty-four-hour-a-day position, and most presidents are not compensated financially for extracurricular activities. A board may have presidents who are very conservative financially and are not desirous or aggressive about the size of their monthly check. The attitude or philosophy of the president should not make a difference. The office is what warrants the high compensation. Most boards permit the salary of a president to remain too low rather than too high.

A second benefit and an important one is that a president should be furnished a residence, which is the presidential manor. Practically all activities that the president will engage in will be related to his role as president. Many a president's home is almost a public thoroughfare. A fairly large residence should be made available on or near the campus. Suitable help can be provided to assist the family in maintaining the inside as well as the outside in proper repair. The dining commons could be authorized to provide the meals as well as service for special dinners and teas which occur so often in the routine of presidential functions.

A third major benefit is that the president should be provided a school car. Most of the mileage that a president accumulates on a car will be for college business. A better than average car is a must and the board can instruct the appropriate authorities to purchase a vehicle. The president entertains potential donors, prominent state dignitaries, alumni, etc., and the car should be large enough to handle special parties comfortably. Some colleges furnish a chauffeur to assist the president, and such a man is the official or one of the official chauffeurs for the college vehicles. A few colleges are purchasing airplanes for the institution, and this is a trend that will have more significance as each year transpires.

A fourth benefit is to make sure that the president does not get stuck with out-of-pocket expenses. The little day-by-day expenses can literally bankrupt a president. A board can authorize the business office to set up a liberal expense account for the president. The president will be careful in his use of the expense account. Few will be unwise spenders.

There are other benefits that the board can review which will be money wisely spent to make the president the most capable chief executive that can be selected.

INAUGURATION

A board should decide once they have selected a president what type of inauguration ceremony will be appropriate. There are some difficulties in convoking a ceremony of inauguration. Traditionally held a few months after the president has been in office, it seems after the fact and a bit out of place. A president is placed on the spot in an inauguration address because he is just getting settled in the office and is not ready to make too many major commitments for the institution. The inauguration ceremony can be a significant activity for a college community if it is programmed appropriately. An inauguration is a focusing together and a time of recommitment and dedication to the progress of the institution. It is a period of reidentification and solidification of the institution within and without.

The inauguration should be a ceremony of great dignity and honor, exhibiting the institution at its best. The facilities in which it is held, the manner of the program, the style of the institution, the method of publicity all contribute to setting the proper stage for his acceptance. The inauguration is a time when the institution can put its best foot forward and have a tremendous opportunity for positive public relations. The college has the proper machinery to generate a memorable and impressive inauguration. If an appropriate facility of culture and dignity is not present on your campus, then rent a more adequate setting from a facility in your community. If neither are available then you must do the best you can.

REFORMER OR INNOVATOR

The president must decide what type of emphasis he will employ during his term as president. Some institutions may desire the chief executive to transform the institution back to some of its original policies. There are a number of boards which have publicly stated that their institution has made too many radical changes and who are desirous of returning it to its former status. If a president is placed in that position by the board he is to be pitied. Regression is not complimentary to higher education and he will be going against the grain to undo the advances that have been made. A president becomes a "hatchet man" when he must work to modify policies and eradicate attitudes or events that have deeply concerned the board. This is not to rule out moderation and return to original policies. The course chosen by a college may have been detrimental, costly, improper, and the need to modify is highly validated.

Reforms are to be instituted only after careful review, research, and recommendation. Reforms that are necessary to the future of education and the institution are to be wholeheartedly supported. Reforms that are an outgrowth of suspicion, fear, and unreliable information have no place in higher education. A president stands in the gap to protect the board and the institution from embarking on improper reforms. Paradoxically, the president may be hired to be the force behind institutional innovation. He himself may not be an innovator but can put the wheels in motion to generate new and exciting innovation. A dynamic institution will have a dynamic president who is a supporter of innovation. Higher education to perform to its maximum capacity should be the prime example of innovation throughout the world. Innovation can demand a high price in facilities and salaries and be a source of consternation to a board. An institution that is willing to have quality needs innovation. Innovation to be implemented needs a wise chief executive.

INTERPRETER

The chief executive is the interpreter of the institution to a variety of publics. The task of formulating policies is critical and demands considerable attention from the president. Adequate policies are the oil for the machinery of higher education. The president is the main spokesman for the institution. It is incumbent that the chief executive be a man gifted in the art of articulation so that he can enunciate ably the goals and purposes of the institution. The president by virtue of his office is ex officio chairman of all committees within the institution. The president should decide what committees are most crucial to major policy decisions and innovations. In interpreting the institution, the president has two concerns—formulation and enunciation. How he formulates policies will determine the method of enunciation and interpretation. As chief executive he will be called upon to deliver at least twenty major speeches a year plus a myriad of minor speaking assignments. All of these are time-consuming and should be carefully prepared for presentation. Too often presidents speak out of their hip pocket or off the top of their head, and their audiences are keenly aware of it. Many a president can remember nightmares that have resulted from inadequate presentation of speeches. A president should employ the appropriate individuals to assist him in speech preparation. When a president speaks, he speaks for the institution and carries its full authority. Sloppy and poor presentation does not reflect wise judgment. It is better for the president to decline a speaking engagement than to deliver it ill-prepared. Once or twice the president can get away with it but not continually. It is true that major themes must run consistently throughout a president's speeches. These themes can be recurring and effective if they are relevant.

TURMOIL

No president or board that governs institutions of higher learning will ever escape turmoil or tension. These things are healthy ingredients in the process of education and are not to be labeled detrimental. A president can, however, be caught in the cross-fire of some of the activities that contribute to tension and stress. The loyalty oath controversy, civil rights, racial conflicts, student unrest, academic freedoms, controversial speakers policy, bargaining groups and unions, salary requests, and codal behavior standards are all facets that may contribute to tension on campuses. In addition, the constituency, the alumni, the legislature and the potential benefactors can create strong pressure that can be nerve-racking for even the most capable college president. A president must simply learn to live with stress and tension. Docile campuses are not too stimulating and can be quite stagnating to innovation. Transition, tension, innovation, and experimentation are all positive signs of a dynamic institution even though they create turmoil on a campus. Boards and presidents that have not experienced conflict and stress may be shattered by this first exposure to healthy conflict. If such tension is programmed constructively it is in the best interests of the institution to pursue it. Presidents and boards should welcome tension, not fear it. It can be the life blood of progress. Tension, however, is not a license for irresponsibility, violence, disruptiveness, and pressures that are detrimental to the orderly pursuit of higher education. Those avenues of conflict that are utilized for personal gain, self-aggrandizement, or political fortune are to be blocked and shut off from gratification in an institution of higher learning. The president must be a master of strategy, patience, and strength for leadership amid turmoil. Presidents who try to squelch positive tension and conflict may unwittingly smother progress. Such suffocation is tragic and must not be condoned.

PROCRASTINATION

A president is faced with many difficult assignments. Some of the assignments are rough and exhausting. A chief executive can be prone to procrastination; he may rationalize difficult assignments when he should not. A president must get the job done as quickly as possible though the responsibilities are tedious, laborious, and difficult. Procrastination is putting off until tomorrow what you had put off to do today. If a president avoids a rough assignment and procrastinates, the task will become even more difficult to accomplish. There is certainly the proper timing for policy implementation, but procrastination can become a regular habit and that type of habituation is fatal for the chief executive to follow. A president can also fall into the trap of rationalizing policies, goals, purposes, and can get involved in a gray area of methodology. The president as chief interpreter of the institution naturally follows trains of rationalization in his communication. If he is not careful, rationalization can paint a picture of a president speaking out of both sides of his mouth. A president must display the utmost honesty and consistency to those both within and without the institution. A president that disregards consistency and honesty and seeks to rationalize his approach is skating on thin ice. Not only may the chief executive be involved in procrastination, rationalization, avoidance or inconsistency, but the most difficult may be the degree of repetition that surrounds his task. A president can be caught up in repetition or routine. Similar faces or committees, standard policies, or similar constituency may become overly repetitious for aggressive leaders. The chief executive must avoid becoming encased in routine or repetition. Presenting the goals of the college two dozen times can be exciting the twenty-fourth time if the president is equipped with the vision for progress and growth.

DELEGATION

A president can either choose to run a one-man show or delegate authority to responsible administrators and committees. There are still a number of presidents who literally run a one-man operation that can have disastrous consequences for the institution. A capable and confident president will utilize his prerogative of delegation wisely and appropriately. The chief executive can delegate to his first-line executive officers such as the provost, deans, business manager, the authority to handle affairs in their areas. A top-level, hard-working executive staff will only strengthen the institution.

A good president will properly delegate and instruct his executive officers in all affairs of the academic enterprise. His desire should be to train people who are as knowledgeable and career-oriented as he. The executive officers should be so trained and equipped through the president's tutelage that they are ready to assume the presidency if need be. A president that is jealous of training his executive officers to be as well-equipped as a president for fear they will take over does not possess the honest values needed for his office. Five top executive officers are better than one top man with four weak executives.

As an institution grows the president is incapable of handling the multifaceted vectors of the institution. It is essential that the offices and businesses of the institution be managed wisely, and this is where delegation is a key. Of course, the president may not be able to train his executive officers because they do not have the personnel equipped to do the job, in which case he must handle more of the affairs himself. If a president has weak line officers they should be changed. More than any other corporation, the academic enterprise is guilty of perpetuating weakness. A president must be cognizant of weakness and demand improvement. If a board is aware of this weakness administrationally, they can take the most appropriate measures to eliminate them. Delegation should be characterized by quality and simplicity. Cumbersome organization and mediocre performance are not beneficial for the growth of an institution. Quality is a standard that should be the norm. Simplicity is a style that can produce efficiency.

PUBLIC RELATIONS AND DEVELOPMENT

The president is actually the chief public relations officer and the chief development officer of the institution. There may be others appointed with these titles but in actuality the president is responsible for their adequate functioning. A president may not have the experience or the ability to be a supersalesman but in the areas of development potential donors regard the president as the key in their negotiation. Most benefactors want to see the top man before they give a major gift to an institution. The president carries with his office a tremendous amount of honor, respect, prestige, and some individuals stand in awe of his position. Before a major gift is donated, a philanthropist might say, "I want to talk to the president and hear his view of the future of the college." The presidential role implies verity of thought; therefore, the potential donor believes that what the president says is valid.

Public relations is a vital and integral phase of a college program. The president realizes more than other persons the need for adequate and efficient public relations. Every person employed at an institution is a spokesman in a public relations sense, either positive or negative. The president sits at the top as the prime mover and interpreter of public relations. The acts of a student, the political activities of a faculty, and demonstrations or controversial events are all public relation vehicles. The president can develop into a skilled tactician in public relations. Programs should not be compromised because the public relations value is a danger in some institutions. The president as chief public relations officer earns his money when he interprets particular positions that otherwise may be regarded suspiciously by the public.

Any college or university needs a strong development program, and a good president will give a strong share of his time to it. Many, many academias buckle under the responsibility of development which is a never ending task. A president should seek to employ the best development officer he can find. A top development officer will return the expenditure of his operation manyfold.

EROSION OF POWER

Presidents have power. How they exercise that power may well determine their success or failure at an institution. The president's method will be either bureaucratic, autocratic, idiocratic, or democratic. The style of power may be determined by the need of the institution. The democratic approach envisions the most ideal style and integrates a "quarterback philosophy." The pronoun in the frame of reference is "we." The orientation is group centered. The motivation is the group and recognition of them. The objectives are to promulgate the consensus of the group and to develop the purpose of the group. The contact with the employees is frequent and the demands of the employees are exhibited through cooperation. The communication is by interaction and is never a one-way street. The morale of the institution is high because of intrgrative and teamwork attitudes. Presidents as well as boards can see these prerogatives of power eroded by default more than anything else. Neglect of major concerns and attention to other pressing needs may eradicate presidential prowess in power and policy making. The president must ever be careful that people are not manipulated or antagonized unnecessarily. His display of authority must not involve superficial commitments or ambitions. Because power can corrupt, the president must seek to utilize the wisest approach else he becomes a dictator. Dictatorship has no place in a democratic structure of higher learning.

BOARD MEETINGS

The president is a key factor in the board meetings. His task will be to ensure the development of an appropriate agenda and insure the board's attention to the most advantageous items for review. The board meetings are not to be arenas for fighting but to be symposiums for confrontations.

A president is the "real" chairman who sees that the meetings function efficiently and effectively. The board chairman most often is nominally in charge of the meeting, but the president more than not prepares the materials for discussion. A president is the chief spokesman for the institution and must be able to articulate its nature to the board. A board looks to the president for leadership, counsel, and direction, and must be capable of giving such to the board in its regularly convened meetings. The president is the one person that interacts more often with the board than any other person. Most of his contacts will be through meetings of committee or full board. He must assist the board chairman in the style of meeting so that the board meeting is utilized to its maximum potential. The president can serve as the salt that preserves the best flavor of the meetings. Some board meetings have ended in chaos, dissension, and long-remembered ill feelings. The president always strives to keep the chairman guiding the meeting at an even keel with objectivity and positiveness prevailing. Well-organized and carefully prepared meetings are essential. Poorly called and improperly structured meetings are time-consuming and disruptive. A president and the board chairman are chartered to set the regular meetings at a time expedient for all. The date should be at convenient hours and period that can be best for maximum efficiency.

ENFORCED RESIGNATIONS

A board of trustees may request a president to resign. It is regrettable when this occurs, but a number of college presidents have been invited to terminate their positions. Such a practice will continue though it may receive lesser attention in the future. Enforced resignations seldom transpire unexpectedly. The president usually is aware that trouble is brewing and that his resignation is considered to be forthcoming. When such enforced resignations occur at major universities it is front-page news, and is embarrassing both to the president and to the institution. Enforced resignations initiated over controversial policies can have a lasting effect on an institution. Some colleges may be side-tracked for many years because of a controversial resignation, and many qualified teachers may shy away from the institution for fear of personal reprisal.

A board should never require a forced resignation unless it is their final alternative. This approach seldom is in the best interests of higher education and may place an indelible black mark on that institution. The president, however, must realize he is responsible for what transpires within an institution and must ever be ready to stand in its defense. The chief executive may well be the whipping boy for the trustees and must accept that fact when he becomes president. Some boards may graciously promote a president to chancellor in recognition of his long and faithful service. If a board chooses to do this it must carefully spell out the new president's responsibilities or you will have a duality of leadership. Duality cannot bring unanimity.

SUMMARY

The president must have a clear conception of the function of education in a democratic society. This is basic if he is to lead an academic enterprise. Faulty understanding will lead him to choose unwise and improper paths for his institution. The understanding of the function of education will determine the methods he will employ in the day-to-day decision-making process. Because the role of education changes in modern society, the president must have the capacity to adjust and grow with it. Those who are looking for an easy job are not suited for the presidency. This is where the action takes place in higher education and men of courage and strength are the norm. The president is obligated to maintain a relationship of objectivity coupled with understanding regarding the board. Individual board members must succeed in knowing their president so that there may be solidification of dedication and identification of goals. A deep understanding will help smooth the many and varied rough spots an institution must go through. It is mandatory that a president understand his board and be able to anticipate its reactions. The board and the president are practical strategists, striving together to achieve the best combinations for success in their institution. There must never develop a battle line between the board and the president. If the relationship is one of battles and wars, then progress is stifled. Battle scars testifying to conflicts between president and board are not in the best interests of the academic community.

The internal organization wants to sense that their top representative is on the best relations with the board and that the harmony of the president and board permeates the heart-beat of the institution. Strained feelings between the two top authoritative agencies must be eliminated and the climate of cohesive understanding projected and diffused. It is important that the board give the president flexibility in which to maneuver. An attitude by the board that the president is working for them and they will therefore tell him what to do is hardly the correct stance. Such a posture develops only puppet administrators—a situation that is dangerous to higher education. Some boards still may choose to operate with this philosophy and such boards should be cautioned.

The board and president will not always agree and should not. The confidence established between the two will permit diverse interaction that is a part of the growth of a dynamic institution. Presidents are to be watchful of internalizing unwarranted fears of the board.

If a president generates fear of the board then the results are a timid president, with insipid and inactive leadership.

An alert chief executive will train a staff and execute a program to handle the daily affairs of an institution. He will support his staff and give them the authority and confidence to perform their tasks. They will perform to their maximum capabilities in this type of atmosphere. If his staff develops and grows professionally, then those that seek their counsel will gain satisfaction from going to these appropriately delegated members. This alleviates cumbersome and unnecessary activities for the president and satisfies the needs of the internal operation.

In the performance of presidential duties the chief executive needs to gather a consensus from his board, faculty, students, alumni, and public generally as to what the goals of the institution are. His task then is to determine the best methods of making progress toward those goals. Remembering he is the elected agent of representation, he strives always for true consensus. He does not try to sell his notions, though he may suggest alternatives. The president is the catalyst and the perpetuator of consensus. This is the highest type of leadership.

Here is an illustration of the duties of the president as defined in the bylaws of the University of Mississippi:

Article IX

HEADS OF INSTITUTIONS

1. The Chancellor or President of each of the several state institutions of higher learning shall be responsible for the administration of the several divisions and departments of his institution and for keeping its expenditures strictly in harmony with the budgetary authorizations of the Board and within the limitations provided therein.

2. The Chancellor or President shall have the initiative in shaping the education policy and academic standards of his institution, in recommending such policy to the Board and in maintaining it, subject to final policy revisions made by the Board.

3. The Chancellor or President shall have the initiative in the selection and recommendation for election by the Board of all employees and faculty members of his institution; and he shall have authority to fill vacancies that occur as emergencies, when the salary outlay is within the budget appropriations provided for such positions, all subject to authority for review and rejection or approval by the Board of Trustees, in which body rests the sole power of election and confirmation or rejection of all appointments.

4. The Chancellor or President is charged with the responsibility for maintaining appropriate standards of conduct of students, and is authorized to expel, dismiss, suspend and place limitations on continued attendance and to levy penalties for disciplinary violations, subject to procedures of due process.

QUESTIONS

1. What type of educational and personal qualifications are necessary for a college president?
2. Describe the nature of the relationship that should be evident between the president and the governing board.
3. Analyze the role of the president and the main elements that describe it.
4. What factors hinder the president from performing at his greatest potential?
5. How can the effectiveness of the president be adequately and reliably measured?
6. Is the office of the president necessary for institutions of higher learning? Why?
7. Indicate the most important factors that a board should consider in the selection of a new president.

BIBLIOGRAPHY

COWLEY, WILLIAM H. "What Does a President Do?," an address presented at the inauguration of Roy E. Lieuallen as president of Oregon College of Education (February 5, 1959).

DONOVAN, HERMAN L. "The Changing Conception of the College Presidency," *Association of American Colleges Bulletin* (March, 1957), pp. 44–45.

DODDS, HAROLD W. *The Academic President—Educator or Caretaker?* New York: McGraw-Hill, 1962.

EBIN, PAUL N. "College President on a Tightrope," *College and University Business*, XXVII, No. 4 (October 1958), p. 21.

FLEXNER, ABRAHAM. *I Remember.* New York: Simon and Schuster, 1940.

HUTCHINS, ROBERT M. "The Administrator: Leader or Officeholder," *Journal of Higher Education*, XVI, No. 8 (November 1946).

———. "The Administrator Reconsidered: University and Foundation," 1955, *Freedom, Education and the Fund, Essays and Address, 1946–1956.* New York: Meridian Books, 1956.

JAMES, HENRY. *Charles W. Eliot, President of Harvard University, 1869–1909.* Boston, Mass.: Houghton Mifflin, 1930.

LOWELL, LAWRENCE A. *What A University President Has Learned.* New York: Macmillan, 1938.

PRAETOR, RALPH. *The College President,* The Center for Applied Research in Education, Inc., Washington, D.C., 1963.

ROBB, FELIX C. "An Open Letter to a New College President," *College and University Business* (February 1962), pp. 35–38.

SAMMARTINO, PETER. *The President of a Small College.* Rutherford, N.J.,: Fairleigh Dickinson College Press, 1954, pp. 12–132.

SCHMIDT, GEORGE P. *The Old Time College President.* New York: Columbia U.P., 1930.

SELDON, WILLIAM K. "How Long is a College President?," *Liberal Education,* The Bulletin of the Association of American Colleges, XLVI, No. 1 (March 1960), pp. 5–15.

SELZNICK, PHILIP. *Leadership in Administration.* New York: Harper, 1957.

STEPHENS, RICHARD W. "The Academic Administrator, The Role of the University President," Doctoral Dissertation, University of North Carolina, Chapel Hill, N.C., 1956.

STOKE, HAROLD W. *The American College President.* New York: Harper, 1959.
TEAD, ORDWAY. *The Art of Leadership.* New York: McGraw-Hill, 1935.
"Tentative Thoughts Concerning Desirable Qualifications for a University
    President," unpublished draft approved by the Academic Senate Advisory
    Committee on the Selection of a President, Berkeley, April 9, 1957.
WRESTON, HENRY M. *Academic Processions, Reflections of a College President.*
    New York: Columbia U.P., 1959.

CHAPTER 4

Organizing the Board of Trustees[1]

THE GOVERNING BOARD AND PHILOSOPHY OF EDUCATION

It is estimated that for the next few years new colleges will open at the rate of one per week, so great is the demand in America for higher education. Education is already the largest industry in the nation. Every American pays money in support of higher education. The persons entrusted with the responsibility for the proper disbursement of the huge sums needed to finance higher education are the trustees.

In light of the trustees' great responsibility for proper handling of large sums, it is paradoxically true that there is a persistent and probably growing feeling that higher education is drifting toward purposelessness and lack of direction. Educational facilities and enrollments are increasing at dramatic rates, but these are insufficient to stifle the nagging doubts as to the ultimate value of the whole business. In short, there seems to be a haziness in the understandings of matters of educational philosophy. The Danforth report on church colleges speaks about this "lack of philosophical depth" and says, "The church institutions are floundering in this respect, as is higher education at large." Robert Hutchins, former president of the University of Chicago, writes frequently about this dilemma in his syndicated newspaper column, "What Kind of World?"

This issue of educational philosophy, which is what gives distinctiveness to a school, may seem to have the most immediate relevance for private schools. Private education today costs so much more to the student than public education that it is essential for private schools to convince their prospective students that they offer something unique—something that cannot be obtained at a less expensive school, something that is worth the extra money. Thus the crisis of identity is probably more vital at private schools than at public schools.

[1] Orley R. Herron, "Trustees Should Lead Search for Philosophy of Education," *College and University Business Journal*, Vol. 43, No. 8 (February 1968).

However, the question of educational philosophy is not reserved for trustees at private schools. State schools too must know what they are about. Of course, part of their uniqueness is determined by the fact that their function is to serve their particular state. But with the high degree of mobility among Americans today, state schools cannot afford to be too insular or provincial in their educational concerns. One of the basic unresolved questions of educational philosophy today is whether the university should provide a technically trained labor force or merely intellectual development for the individual. Or is it possible to provide both? What kind of academic program would be best suited to produce the one, and what kind would likely produce the other? Also, what should be the relationship between departments? Is it proper to allow departments to be as isolated as they are now on most large university campuses? What does this situation say about our concept of truth? What does it say about our concept of man? What of our concept of the educated man? What kind of graduate is this condition likely to produce? What is the proper balance between teaching and research at a university? What happens to a faculty and school when promotions are awarded strictly on the basis of published research? A few such questions make it clear that matters of educational philosophy are vital issues for all colleges and universities, whether private or public.

But what about the role of the trustee in relation to philosophy of education? How concerned with and involved in the matter of educational theory should a board become? Let us notice certain introductory premises.

First, it is obvious that every school has an educational philosophy. That is, there is some reason for doing what is being done at a given institution. Perhaps the educational philosophy is confused, perhaps different elements of the academic community are pulling in opposite directions at some schools; but there is some governing idea (or ideas) behind the functioning of the school, even if it is only a hash of confusion of contradiction.

Second, the educational philosophy of a school is the real heart of that institution. The ideas behind the school are what give it reason for being. All other aspects of the institution must reflect its educational philosophy. Every decision made by a dean relative to new faculty appointments must be made in the light of the institution's overall purpose. The same must be said for every decision made by a governing board. Thus, it may be more illuminating to speak of governing ideas than to speak of governing boards.

Third, since educational philosophy is central, it is not enough to say that every school has an educational philosophy. For if it is chaotic or hazily understood, it can be detrimental to the functions of the school.

What is needed is a coherent philosophy; not only coherent, but articulated so well that all members of the academic community will be able to understand it.

Fourth, if this matter of educational philosophy is as central as the author maintains, it is much too important for the trustees to ignore. A governing board is not doing its job properly if it concerns itself exclusively, or even primarily, with the externals of the institution. And in comparison to the matter of educational philosophy, the matters of budgets and buildings, important as they are to higher education, are externals. They are the external channels through which the school seeks to achieve its educational purposes.

Since this question of educational philosophy is too crucial for governing boards to ignore, let us notice a few of the problems connected with the relationship between the governing board and educational philosophy.

The first problem in this relationship is connected with the personnel who compose the board. In fact, this problem is the seminal one; the other ones grow out of it. Many board members are chosen because of their financial interests and abilities. Often these trustees do not have a college education themselves. These board members are needed for their business advice, but they often do an unsatisfactory job of dealing with matters of educational philosophy.

Because of this prevalent condition among governing boards, it is sad but true that the trustee is often the member of the college family who knows the least about the subject of philosophy of education. When this is true, it is difficult for the president, other administrators, and faculty members (and perhaps even students) not to take a condescending attitude toward the trustees. This condescension exhibits itself in the board meetings when the president explains as much of the educational philosophy of the college as is necessary to obtain trustee approval of a particular program—and no more. Many presidents feel that one of their most difficult jobs is to educate the trustees in matters of education. Probably many more have given up on the idea of educating trustees, and they try to keep the subject of educational philosophy from coming up any more than necessary, feeling that trustees are not interested in such theoretical matters. In either case, the president has taken (of necessity) a condescending attitude toward the board.

The lack of understanding of educational philosophy on the part of trustees leads to an ironic situation. Supposedly the board hires the president to be an executive; he is to handle the practical working out of the board's policies. But in actual fact most boards show more interest in practical details—the externals, as we have called them—than in matters of policy. Trustees seem more interested in questions of "how" than in questions of "why." They seem to have ceded to administrators by default the more basic task of determining matters of educational philosophy while retaining for themselves the lesser tasks of educational procedure.

As long as the governing board neglects the area of educational philosophy, it will have no clear-cut criterion for determining the propriety of the various proposals brought to it for action. The board will have no systematic method of checking the step-by-step progress of the school. It will lack the basic criterion for such vital decisions as whom to select for the presidency and on what basis to appeal for support.

One more problem to be mentioned is the amount of time needed to become a serious student of education. Admittedly, this is a serious problem and one for which there is no easy answer. It must simply be said that the position of trustee is not an honorary one. The trustee who takes his position seriously must be willing to devote time to it. There is just no short-cut.

These, then, are some of the problems involved in the relation of governing boards to governing ideas. For the trustee who wants to take seriously the heavy but essential burden of working through the educational philosophy of his institution, the following is a checklist of questions which you should ask yourself:

1. Can you state the philosophy of education which governs your school?

2. Can you describe the essential differences between your school and that similar one not many miles away?

3. Does the Education Committee of the board ever talk educational philosophy? Or does it take up its time with practical and procedural matters, the "nuts and bolts"?

4. Does the full board ever discuss educational philosophy?

5. Does either the Education Committee or the full board regularly review the educational philosophy of the institution? Is the matter listed on the formal agenda?

6. What qualifications and background does your board require for the chairman of the Education Committee?

7. Do you have a broad representation of the academic community consulting regularly with the Education Committee of the board?

8. Whatever the philosophy of education at your school happens to be, how did it come into being?

9. In your institution, who decides matters of educational philosophy? Who holds the real power for charting the course of the school?

10. Are such matters as faculty recruiting, faculty promotion, student recruiting, budgetary expenditures, and building needs determined in the light of a clearly delineated philosophy of education?

For those trustees who are not entirely satisfied with their answers to the preceding questions, the author offers the following recommendations for your consideration:

1. It is recommended that each board contain some members of the professional educational community. These persons should be administrators or faculty members from other campuses who understand and sympathize with the philosophy of education of your institution. Educators should be given assignments on the Education Committee of the board and are likely candidates for the chairmanship of the committee.

2. It is recommended that the need for men with an understanding of matters of educational theory be kept in mind whenever new board members are sought, even when the situation calls for the choice of a person who is not a professional educator.

3. It is recommended that administrators and faculty members be consulted regularly for their counsel on matters of educational philosophy. It is in no way meant to imply that the thinking of those educators in the employ of an institution should be ignored by the trustees.

4. It is recommended that the governing board be convened for a session devoted entirely to the question of the educational philosophy of the institution. If the board has allowed the college to drift in some haphazard fashion, then the board must begin at once to provide leadership and direction for its institution. It must spell our clearly the long-range aims and objectives which it desires to see implemented.

5. Once the long-range aims and objectives are clearly enunciated, the author recommends that the board place as a regular item on its agenda the review of those goals. The need for a regular review is especially important for our time, since change occurs very rapidly.

6. As a governing board assumes its proper role of determining matters of educational philosophy, it must be very careful to make smooth transition in whatever changes it causes in the power structure of the institution. Administrators will shift from a legislative to an advisory and executive capacity. Any shift must be explained clearly. Observe and caution against seeming arrogant or power-hungry individuals. The advice of top administrators is invaluable and should be prized at all times, certainly during times of transition.

7. A warning against imitativeness must be sounded. Imitating prestige schools is too often the method chosen by trustees to solve quickly and easily matters of educational theory as they apply to their particular school. Imitation can be devastatingly deadly, as when a private school merely tries to mimic a top-flight public university program. After all, a student is likely to ask, why spend the extra money only to receive the same thing? But imitation can be stifling in a broader manner. If part of the genius of American higher education lies in its diversity, the more

imitation there is, the less diversity. Creative thinking is always much more difficult than imitation, but it is also more enriching and rewarding.

Since much money and faith are being placed in higher education and since governing ideas are vitally important, governing boards do indeed have a heavy responsibility to be involved in philosophy of education. The author trusts that trustees will take seriously their important positions and remove any haziness and uncertainty that may exist about the direction which higher education is to take. Be leaders in education, not followers.

SELECTING BOARD MEMBERS[2]

Governing boards occupy the strategic command posts in higher education. In a great sense, they direct, command, rule, advise, and guide the machinery of the educational enterprise. If they are to lay claim to such pivotal positions of power, then higher education must be assured that the most qualified individuals are being selected as trustees. Research indicates that trustees are selected for membership by one of the four methods: (1) election, (2) appointment, (3) co-optation, (4) ex-officio selection. The prevailing method of selecting board members among privately controlled institutions is by co-optation, and that among publicly controlled colleges the model practice is through appointment by elected state officials. Realizing the remarkably complex role the trustee position requires, the author recommends three basic considerations to be utilized as procedural methods in trustee selection.

First and foremost, examine your present selection policy for trustees and see if it has loopholes that are perpetuating weaknesses. Many selection policies are inadequate and must be revised if an institution is to meet the challenge of this generation. These outdated policies may have been sufficient for earlier days but inadequate for today. Don't permit policies to function if they hinder your institution. Too often these policies are neglected because the trustee member is swamped with responsibilities that appear to demand greater attention. Appoint a committee to review present membership policy and secure the legal and professional advice required to make the most thorough judgment of it.

Secondly, create a membership committee for new board members. The committee should be composed of representatives of the board of trustees, administration, and faculty. It is alarming that most governing boards function in America without the proper checks-and-balance system. There are those individuals who seek positions of power for gain of self, prosperity, or influence for friends and relatives. These individuals

---

[2] Orley R. Herron, "How to Know a Good Trustee—When You Find One," *College and University Business Journal*, Vol. 43, No. 5 (November 1967).

are not to be selected for board membership, but some will be unless there is an adequate screening body.

This membership committee can review thoroughly all potential candidates for board membership and then recommend eligible individuals to the appropriate officials.

Thirdly, create advisory boards for the institution which can also serve as a pool for potential board members. Most institutions have committees such as the President Club, The Board of Reference, The Special 100, etc. Most of them are geared to assist the college in a variety of ways. These committees can be great sources for future board members. The members of these honorary bodies receive an understanding of the institution, and also have the opportunity to demonstrate capabilities that may have gone unnoticed before. Equally as important, these committees of trustees can bring to light weaknesses of potential board members which must be corrected if they are to make a maximum contribution as a full-fledged trustee.

Utilize these committees as "boot camps" for potential trustees. There is nothing more important than selecting or appointing a trustee already oriented, experienced, and dedicated to the aims and objectives of your institution. Remember, there is no substitute for experience, and experience must be evident at the board level.

BASIC STEPS IN ORGANIZATION

There is no college in the United States that does not desire a strong and capable board of trustees. Yet anyone engaged in research relative to boards of trustees finds that many boards are structured and organized in ways that decrease their effectiveness. Though these weaknesses in structure and organization may not be very apparent to those serving on the board, they can be detected through an in-depth analysis and survey. If a college desires a stronger board of trustees, the author suggests the following steps and considerations.

The first and foremost step is to select trustees who are willing to serve. A trustee position requires, by definition, a combination of time, talent, and money. Trustees should be selected who have the ability, the time, and the talent to give to the school. Too often trustees are selected because of the prestige or financial backing they can bring to the institution. I have no quarrel with this type of selection so long as the other needs of the school are not compromised to attract such trustees. Balanced representation is essential.

An ideal member would be one that has the educational background, the executive experience, and the prestige to strengthen a board. In addition, trustees should be selected who want to serve willingly, give liberally, lead positively, and understand perceptively the tasks they are to undertake. They should be the pilots of the ship and must be willing to serve gladly in such a capacity!

The second step is to organize the board with appropriate officers. The officers of the board can consist of a chairman, a vice-chairman, a secretary, a treasurer, and any designated assistants or other officers that may be deemed necessary for the board. Each member serving as an officer can hold office until his successor is elected or his termination of office or membership on the board expires. The duties of office must be clearly defined and compensation for their responsibilities approved by the board. Examples of job descriptions are contained in the bylaws of three institutions included in the appendix.

The third step is to organize the board on a committee basis. The average size of a board of trustees is approximately twenty members. A board of this size should be broken down into six basic committees: the education committee, the finance committee, the building committee, the development and long-range planning committee, the student services committee, and the membership committee. In addition to these committees, an executive committee should be formed, composed of the chairman of each committee plus the chairman of the board. This executive committee can be authorized to function as the full board when expediency and distance necessitate their action. The president should meet regularly with the committee chairmen to assist them in becoming knowledgeable and decisive leaders.

The chairman of the board and the president of the college must permit the committees to review all policy matters concerning their committee responsibilities. They should also make certain that decisions involving any of the committees' jurisdictions are reviewed initially by the appropriate committee for a report at a later meeting.

Reports given by a committee to the full board should be submitted in writing. Written reports will ensure a greater probability of avoiding digressions and disruptions that can be very costly at a full board meeting.

The president of the institution can provide secretarial staff for the board members to assist them in completing written reports. Committee assignments may be changed to orient a board to the total program of the college.

The fourth major step is to correlate the skills and assignments of the board members with their qualifications. Sometimes board members are given responsibilities which they may not be able to complete or which at best will be extremely difficult for them to fulfill. Remember that board members are human and need to have the taste of success. A trustee may become discouraged because of an inappropriate assignment, and this could be detrimental to a college's potential. It is essential that you match the tasks and abilities of the trustees together and make sure the trustee understands exactly what is to be accomplished. The matching of skills and tasks will take careful planning, but this will build a stronger institution and, of course, a stronger board.

A major consideration is that the meetings of the board should be called only when it is necessary. This statement seems perfectly obvious, yet it is constantly violated by many administrators. There are by-laws that require boards of trustees to meet at regularly designated times on the yearly calendar. These meetings of the board, however regular or irregular they may be, must be carefully planned, programmed, and structured. Every person is selfish of his time and the board is a high-priced corporation that should require maximum utilization of trustee man-hours. Don't call meetings which are not worthy of the board's attention, consideration and time. A college that involves a board in picayune details and matters best handled by delegation to the administration and faculty is bound to have problems. Always ask, Is the meeting necessary? If not, don't call it! A constant criticism by board members is the calling of meetings that were neither essential, pertinent, nor necessary.

The last equally important consideration is that all boards have a mandatory retirement age for trustees. The college should have some means of "graduating" board members once they have reached a certain age. A "trustee emeritus" position can be created so that once a trustee retires he can always serve as a "trustee emeritus." This position can have dignity and prestige, and can be quite beneficial for an institution. Trustees who have an emeritus designation can attend meetings but would be ineligible to vote. A proper age for mandatory retirement is seventy.

In addition to this, the membership committee should review the appointments of trustees yearly if the board is a self-perpetuating unit. This can provide a checks-and-balance system for the board. It should be noted that some colleges have trustees the administrators desire to retire before a specific mandatory age. The reasons for this are often varied and even quite controversial. Here again, policies that provide for a review of membership and a gracious method of "retiring trustees" early could be extremely helpful for all concerned. Admittedly, this does not deal with the problem of boards that have terms of sixteen years for trustees as in some major public institutions. Later in the series this problem will be answered as the focus will be boards of trustees of public colleges and universities.

In conclusion, it can be reiterated that trustee boards are important and equally vital is the need to structure and organize them for maximum effectiveness.

FIVE CHARACTERISTICS OF SUCCESSFUL TRUSTEES[3]

There is certainly no magical formula for the successful operation of institutions or their successful administration by trustees. Yet, there are very vivid and strong attributes that characterize excellence in a college governing board. Five characteristics that the author has observed in successful boards of trustees are as follows:

Occupational Diversity

Variegated occupational distribution among board membership is a key to strength. The institutions that are striving to maintain a balanced occupational diversity in their governing boards are on the right track; this balance will bring forth fruitful results in the future. Steps must be taken to ensure a wide distribution of occupations among the board. Remember, boards have a tendency to become occupationally homogeneous if guidelines are not carefully spelled out.

An institution should delineate its objectives and define the needs to actualize those objectives. A board may be necessitated to reorganize its membership structure for this purpose. Guidelines for new membership, terminal procedures, or reduced or increased membership may be methods utilized to maintain diversity in occupations at the board level.

Executive Experience

Education is a gigantic business. The expenditures in the field of education increase yearly. The management of these expenditures is vested in the trustees. For many universities and colleges, the management requirements are equal to or greater than those of some of the largest corporations in the country.

I submit that unless governing boards are represented by members who are experienced top-level management executives then that institution may not be equal to the phenomenal growth that stands ahead. There are experienced executives who could make valuable contributions to an institution waiting to serve. It is the task of an institution to discover who and where they are. The development staff of a college should have an entrée to many such individuals if it is doing the task it is commissioned to perform. Research has demonstrated very clearly that leaders in particularly successful management enterprises have the background to become successful trustees.

Education

It cannot be overemphasized that trustees who chart the destiny of an academic community must be educationally equipped for the job.

[3] *Ibid.*

Sound and complex decisions cannot be expertly exercised unless there is an educational framework to rely upon. The level of sophistication of knowledge is changing so rapidly that it is going to take the wisest educational know-how to guide an institution of higher learning satisfactorily.

A board must recruit and select the finest top-level management team of administrators available to assist them in expediting decisions called for in this school. It is true that not every board member has to be equipped with a Ph.D. However, each individual trustee must be capable of and available for advising and consulting with the rest of the board on the multifaceted problems of their institution.

Availability

The most common agreement among writers and consultants relative to qualifications of board members is that the expectation of persons selected for membership is based on the assumption that they will have the time to devote to their duties.

Lack of time or failure to take time for the work is often the reason why a trustee proves inadequate. Select trustees who can give time to their responsibilities. A board cannot afford to have trustees who are always "too busy" to devote sufficient time to the academic mission.

A board may select a few top-corporation executives, however, who will bring prestige to an institution because of their managerial position. It must be noted, though, someone still must assume his responsibility as trustee until he has the time to give to the board. A board should have diversity of geographical representation, yet have a membership that can physically meet in a central location when essential. Distance, time and money (because many schools do not pay expenses of trustees) can be limiting factors. The executive committee of the board must be residentially located to convene very regularly if need be.

Motivation

Many studies have been undertaken relative to the general topic of motivation. Though these studies have made a significant impact upon the field of education they have shed little light on how to motivate a board of trustees. Governing boards must be motivated if they are to produce to their maximum capability. Research has indicated that individuals who have children in school have a greater motivation than those who do not. Equally as important is the fact that those who live in the same residential community of the institution they serve are more motivated than those who reside outside of it.

If a board is highly motivated, its efforts will have tangible rewards. If a board, however, is lethargic, apathetic, and not motivated, the institution will reflect that characteristic loudly and clearly. That reflection will not be positive and progressive, but one that produces detrimental consequences.

Your board should possess to a strong degree the five basic characteristics: occupational diversity, executive experience, education, availability, and motivation. If or when it does, you have the beginnings of success.

THE AGE OF BOARD MEMBERS[4]

Some trustees may simply be too old for the job. The average date of graduation from college of trustees serving today is 1924. These statements may seem to be dramatic, but in a recent survey conducted by the author covering 1,016 board of trustee members representing 57 colleges and universities, approximately 87 percent of the trustees were age forty-one or older. Strikingly apparent was the fact that almost 50 percent of the 1,016 trustees were over age fifty-one, and 37 percent of *that* 50 percent were sixty-one or older.

The institutions surveyed would serve as a sample of colleges and universities in the United States. One can safely conclude that the results would be similar for a larger scale of trustee population.

The author submits that this age distribution of trustee members should be altered to provide a better balance among board members.

It has been common practice to relate age with maturity and experience, the assumption being that those who have lived a greater number of years have more of the kind of experience necessary for wise decision making. It would also be assumed that those individuals who are older have the time, money, and community respect to qualify them for board membership.

The author does not argue with these assumptions. He feels, however, that in a nation where shortly the average age of half of the population will be twenty-six years, with a college student population averaging twenty years of age, we need to begin thinking young!

It is strongly advocated that no less than 25 percent of the board be represented by members in the 31–40 age bracket, with at least one member in his late twenties.

There are individuals who possess the executive and personal characteristics at those age levels who could bring vision, vigor, and insight to a board of trustees.

Those institutions which have members at the age levels of the late twenties and mid-thirties are extremely well pleased with the performances of such trustees.

[4] Orley R. Herron, "Every Board Should Have One Trustee Under 30," *College and University Business Journal*, Vol. 43, No. 1 (July 1967), pp. 44–46.

All boards of trustees need members that have the ability to get the job done. They need individuals who are mature, perceptive, educated, talented, and "equipped" to meet the challenge of a swiftly changing educational world. In the younger generation are many such people willing and ready to serve.

If your board does not have trustees representing an age level under forty years, you should begin a compaign to recruit such members. If the young members are given the proper orientation and if their skills are matched to the right tasks, your board may well become a model for other institutions to follow.

THE ROLE OF THE CHAIRMAN OF THE GOVERNING BOARD

The chairman of the governing board is the most important person in the authority structure. His executive ability, educational adeptness, and philosophy of power dictate to a great extent the direction a college takes. If he has been given such sweeping and broad powers it is of primary importance to review his office thoroughly. For such an analysis a few general guidelines can be suggested.

First, the chairman of the governing board must be committed to higher education and deeply dedicated to the institution he serves. At the base of this engrossment is the obvious dedication to the development of young people as they set their goals and plan their careers. The unique aspects of the college may circumscribe concepts, beliefs, and norms in the student's development, requiring a sophisticated understanding and sensitivity on the part of the chairman.

The chairman is obligated to realize that his role makes certain demands on his time. With the press of personal business and other activities, he may feel that his time is already limited. But if a man accepts the job of chairman, he must also manage to "find" the time—for example, by curtailing his activities in other organizations that are of less consequence than board chairmanship. A survey of New York college trustees revealed that most boards meet only three times a year, with the average meeting lasting a scant two hours. Between meetings the average trustee devotes less than ten hours a month to the job. Yes most trustees depend upon committees to do the work since they are ill-informed about their college and ill-prepared to make decisions.

As board chairman one has the great responsibility of refraining from expressing one's personal opinions on educational matters. It is of course difficult *not* to speak out on certain issues, yet chairmen have found that as other trustees inquire of his stand on a particular subject, there is really ample opportunity on an informal basis to discuss the merits of any given situation. The board members should constantly seek to avoid a split vote. This isn't always possible, and when time or business urgency needs a decision immediately, one must be ready to give it. In the vast majority of cases, many chairmen believe there must be a 100 percent consensus and avoid a split vote if at all possible. But as chairman he should have courage to ask for a vote even though it may in fact be split— and then support the majority. A chairman should see that everyone has a chance to speak his mind fully on any topic on the agenda; yet as chairman he must also keep the discussion under control. Sometimes this is a fine line to draw, but a chairman must exercise his prerogative when there are expressions irrelevant to the issue at hand, or when enough time has been spent on a subject to justify cutting off further discussion. Of course everyone must have an opportunity to speak, and as chairman it is his privilege to call on people if they are reluctant to speak out on a certain subject, or to have them face their responsibility as a trustee and express an opinion on which they are willing to take a stand, thereby avoiding later criticism that one or more members did not have the opportunity to express their views.

Trustees should stay out of actual administration. Sometimes this is not easy because a man's interest in a certain area will impel him to take decisive action as a trustee in order to get this or that done or to talk to this or that faculty member. In the author's opinion, such a procedure is wrong if it deals with policy or administration, because the administrative personnel must take over on the person-to-person basis. We do not mean that as trustee, and especially as a chairman, one should not be in constant touch with the faculty, staff, and administration, but such contacts can at times be overdone, and keeping trustees out of administration is then likely to become a persistent problem. Trustees—and especially the chairman—should at all times look to the president as the channel of communication through his committees and assistants between staff, faculty, and students.

In addition to presiding at meetings, the chairman should always maintain an open ear as far as the president is concerned. He should hear all opinions, he should expedite those things that need expediting, and call executive committee meetings or board meetings when required. It is the chairman's prerogative to decline to call "unnecessary" meetings or to tell the administration to act on its own judgment on things that perhaps it would rather have the board decide. To draw such a fine line of discrimination often takes skill and discernment. Unnecessary meetings can stifle a board's activity and perhaps even weaken the administration, yet the administration must be wise enough to bring the proper things to the board's attention unless the authority is spelled out in fairly clear fashion. The chairman should be available to the president or any member of the administration who wants to see him at any reasonable hour of day or night.

It is also part of the obligation of the chairman to appear at all major committee meetings. It is true that he should be there as an ex-officio and perhaps nonvoting member, but as such he can keep completely informed of the problems being presented. This procedure certainly helps in making decisions about the future. The chairman should put in an appearance at all campus meetings and gatherings when it is possible to attend, even if held at some distance from the campus; he should be known, available, and active in his support of activities with his presence.

Another major task that the chairman must be ready to accomplish at all times is his "homework." There are a staggering number of reports from and to committees, covering all types of activities on campus. The chairman, of all the trustees, must devote time and attention to them so that he may make intelligent decisions later. It is his major job to keep informed almost on a daily basis if he is to do efficient work.

Today more than ever before is a time of financial testing for colleges. It behooves a chairman to be fully acquainted with the financial principles of the college and, insofar as possible, with the actual details of operation. The selection of a strong finance committee is of vital importance. One who is acquainted with business principles and practices on a firsthand basis is the most promising candidate.

A chairman in many ways sets the pattern for the board personnel. As new members are chosen, they must know the objects of the institution and their attitudes must reflect their most serious beliefs. A chairman and the membership committee should be on the constant lookout for men of similar purposes. Nepotism and favoritism must be avoided at all costs. Actually in selecting new board members, the future of the school and the adherence of its principles are either protected or endangered with every election.

WHAT SOME COLLEGES WANT—AND WHAT THEY GET—IN TRUSTEES[5]

During the recent academic year an exploratory study of the boards of trustees among a selected group of America's colleges was completed. The specific goals of the survey were as follows:

1. To survey the boards of selected colleges to determine the age distribution, formal education, and types of occupations represented by the board members.

2. To determine the quality of leadership provided by the board of trustees as judged by the institution's chief administrative officer.

3. To discover how board members recently appointed compare with those who have served the college for more extended periods.

[5] Orley R. Herron and Ernest Boyer, "What Small Colleges Want—and What They Get—in Trustees," *College and University Business Journal*, Vol, 42, No. 3 (March 1967), pp. 77–79.

Size of Boards

The boards of trustees included in this survey ranged in size from 5 to 35 members. The average size board had 27 members. Table 1 summarizes the data regarding size of boards of trustees at the colleges surveyed.

TABLE 1
Size of Boards of Trustees

Board Membership	Institutions	
	Number	Percent
1–9	8	14.3
10–20	14	25.0
21–30	29	51.8
31	5	8.9

Age of Board Members

The age distribution of board members was investigated. Thirty-nine percent of the board members were between 40 and 50 years of age. Thirty-seven percent were more than 60. Twelve percent of the board members were between the ages of 30 and 40, while 0.6 percent were younger than 30 years (see Table 2).

TABLE 2
Age Distribution of Board Members

Age	Institutions	
	Number	Percent
20–30	6	0.6
30–40	130	12.8
40–50	401	39.5
50–60	104	10.2
60–70	345	34.0
70–Over	30	2.9
Total	1,016	100.0

A difference in the age distribution of board members at accredited and nonaccredited institutions was noted. Although the largest number of board members from accredited institutions averaged 40–50 years old (44.9 percent), the largest number of board members at nonaccredited institutions (37.1 percent) were in the 60–70 age group.

Occupations

The occupations represented on the college boards of trustees were investigated. Findings at the selected colleges are recorded in Table 3.

Clearly business executives numerically dominate the boards at both accredited and nonaccredited institutions included in this survey.

TABLE 3
Occupations of Board Members

Occupations	All Institutions	
	Number	Percent
Business executives	343	32.6
Clergymen	277	26.3
Educators	115	10.9
Financiers	77	7.3
Lawyers	61	5.8
Medical physicians	52	4.9
Politics	9	.8
Other	117	11.4
Total	1,051	100.0

Clergymen rank second. The professional educator, representing only 10.9 percent of the board members for all institutions, ranked third.

More than one-fifth (22 percent) of the board members are alumni of the institutions they serve. The survey also showed that 5 percent of the board members in the colleges responding were women. At the time of the study there were 26 board vacancies in the survey group.

Strengths of the Board

The author investigated the extent to which the chief administrative officer at each college judged that the board of trustees effectively assisted the institution in achieving its goal. The presidents were asked to "list one or more of the major strengths of your board as a governing body." Table 4 summarizes the responses.

TABLE 4
"Strengths" of Boards of Trustees as Judged by the College President

Strengths	All Institutions Frequency
Loyalty, dedication, faithfulness	44
Religious commitment	13
Financial assistance	12
Business knowledge	11
Vision and high goals	9
Understand objectives of institution	8
Determine policy	8
Support administration	7
Wide range of professional interest	4
Know their responsibilities	4
Geographical closeness to college	3
Fund-raising ability	4
Balance of age	1
Knowledge of education	4
Alumni	1

Qualifications Preferred by College Presidents

Presidents of colleges also were asked to indicate qualities they desired in new board members. "What traits did you specifically look for when recruiting candidates for your college?" Table 5 summarizes the responses.

TABLE 5
Qualifications Desired in New Board Members

Qualifications	All Institutions Frequency
Financial ability	38
Interest in higher education	38
Devotion to school	37
Religious commitment	19
Success in field	18
Public relations	21
Leadership ability	10
Time and availability	12
Cooperation	11
Integrity	4
Alumni	2
Legal knowledge	3
Vision	4
Open-mindedness	2
Skill in writing and speaking	1
Cultural background	1
Good health	1

In general, college presidents judge their boards to be strong in such vaguely defined traits as "dedication," "loyalty," "religious commitment" (devotion to the school, for example, ranked twice as high as interest in higher education), and in such pragmatic talents as "financial assistance" and "business knowledge." Conversely, educational competence was rarely noted. "Knowledge of education," for example, was mentioned by four presidents only as a "strength" of members of their boards.

The findings reported in Table 5 suggest that college presidents, if given the opportunity to choose board members without restriction, select men with fund-raising skill plus an interest in and (we presume) a knowledge of higher education. School devotion and religious commitment are given substantially less priority as desired qualifications.

Occupational Traits of Recently Named Board Members

These were the "hoped for" traits as recorded by college presidents. What were the occupations of board members who were actually named to the college board during the tenure of the presidents who filled out the questionnaire? (Incidentally, average tenure of the presidents in this study was eight years.) During this period 569 new board members were placed on the 57 college boards surveyed.

The author investigated the types of trustees actually selected to fill the slots by the presidents themselves. Admittedly, in many instances presidents do not have full freedom in board selection. At times members selected must be alumni; 23.9 percent of the recent appointees were alumni. Others are controlled by denominational appointment, and in still other instances powerful board members see to it in one way or another that they are perpetuated.

Nevertheless, it should be assumed that the college president has *some* influence in board selection, and over the long pull board membership does reflect, at least in part, the values and commitments of the institution's chief administrative officer.

Therefore, each president was asked to report the number of board members added "since you became president," and at the same time record the occupational categories the new members represent. What differences in occupation, if any, were there between recent appointees and the board members the presidents in this sample inherited? A comparison of the "old" and the "new" board members appears in Table 6.

TABLE 6

Occupational Distribution of Original Board Members Compared to Those Selected by College President

Occupations	Original Members		New Members	
	Number	Percent	Number	Percent
Business executives	343	32.6	213	37.4
Clergyman	277	26.3	136	23.9
Educators	115	10.9	64	11.2
Financiers	77	7.3	45	7.9
Lawyers	61	5.8	28	4.9
Medical physicians	52	4.9	23	4.4
Politics	9	0.8	3	0.5
Other	117	11.4	60	10.5
Total	1,051	100.0	572	100.7*

* Figures are slightly more than 100 percent because some persons were counted in more than one category.

Table 6 reveals that differences between the "old" and "new" college board members are not dramatic. As before, business executives dominate and clergymen ranked second. Educators—those particularly skilled in the major thrust of higher learning—ranked third. Only 11.2 percent of the total came from this category.

Financial and business interests were actually more heavily represented by the recent appointments than they were for the total board membership. For the total group, business executives and financiers together accounted for 40 percent of the board membership. However, among the current presidents' appointments, they made up 45 percent of the total.

This preliminary survey suggests that the college board of trustees brings more zeal and devotion than specific professional skill to the task at hand. This, at least, is the college president's perception of the situation. Further, while many board members are "businessmen," the president does not judge them effective as "fund-raisers" or powerful financial assets to the institution.

This preliminary survey also reveals a considerable absence of professional occupations such as law, medicine, and, most significantly, education on the college governing board. This lack of balanced board representation may be judged to be a substantial weakness unless one assumes that boards of trustees are to concern themselves with fiscal matters only, a point of view impossible to execute even if theoretically justified. While college administrators and faculties must assume substantial academic leadership, it seems unreasonable to assume that a college can move to a high level of academic achievement if led by a board unskilled in matters of instruction.

Further, it should be noted that while the presidents participating in this survey heightened education leadership on the board, the trend is not a helpful one, if inferences may be drawn from vocational classifications.

Among the recently appointed board members, business and clergy dominate, comprising 61.3 percent; board members appointed during the recent past were by profession "educators."

The execution of trustee duties calls for an integration of knowledge articulated from many disciplines. The role requires an understanding of diversified theoretical and practical educational concepts, curriculum methodology, student personality and demographic characteristics, financial management, and a host of other academic matters if the progress of the institution of higher learning is to be assured. It seems reasonable to assume that those members selected to direct the destinies of America's colleges reflect both the skills and the diversities required.

SUMMARY

Trustees need to be organized to elicit their maximum effectiveness. The primary consideration is that they understand thoroughly the philosophy of education the college is following. Hazy interpretations of the philosophy may lead to poor decisions. Higher education needs direction and the board has the responsibility to give it direction. Questions can be raised to probe whether a board has a good grasp of the educational philosophy of the institution that they govern.

Governing boards are selected for membership by one of four methods: (1) election, (2) appointment, (3) co-optation, (4) ex-officio selection. Selection policies for trustees are to be examined to determine if there are loopholes in them that are perpetuating weaknesses. Too often the policies are neglected because the trustee member is swamped with responsibilities that appear to demand greater attention.

The basic steps in organizing the board are:

1. Select trustees that are willing to serve.
2. Organize the board with the appropriate officers.
3. Organize the board on a committee basis.
4. Correlate the skills and assignments of the board members with their qualifications.

Important considerations are:

1. Call meetings of the board only when necessary.
2. Set mandatory age of retirement for all trustees.

There is no magic formula for successful institutions and successful trustees. Five characteristics of successful trustees are:

1. Occupational diversity
2. Executive experience
3. Education
4. Availability
5. Motivation

The average college graduation date of trustees serving in 1967 was 1924 which may indicate a two-generation credibility gap. This preponderance of older members can be changed.

A survey of presidents of colleges asked what qualifications they thought trustees should have and how they rated their boards. Their analysis, shown in the accompanying tables, provides some interesting data for review and speculation.

QUESTIONS

1. Why is there a great need for boards to understand the philosophy of education of the institution they govern?
2. What type of selection policy is the wisest for an institution to adopt? Describe its nature in detail.
3. Analyze the steps a board of trustees can follow in organizing itself for maximum effectiveness.

4. Outline the attributes that characterize excellence in a college governing board.
5. What age levels of trustees are ideal for a well-balanced board?
6. Indicate the qualifications from a president's point of view that trustees should have. Rate them by priority.

BIBLIOGRAPHY

BELCHER, DONALD R. *The Board of Trustees of the University of Pennsylvania,* Philadelphia: U. of Pennsylvania Press, 1960.

BELL, LAIRD. "From the Trustees Corner," *Association of American Colleges Bulletin* (1952), pp. 27–51.

BENJAMIN, HAROLD (ed.). *Democracy in the Administration of Higher Education.* New York: Harper, 1950.

BROWN, J. D. "Mr. Ruml's Memo: A Wrong Approach to the Right Problem," *Journal of Higher Education* (November 1959), pp. 412–416.

BRUMBAUGH, AARON J. *Problems of College Administration,* Nashville Methodist Church National Board of Education, 1956.

CARMAN, HARRY J. "Trustees Responsibility in College Administration," address delivered to members of boards of trustees of the colleges and universities of Indiana, *The Associated College of Indiana,* Nov. 24, 1956.

CARY, W. W. "Qualifications and Duties of Trustees." Unpublished paper. Asbury College (mimeo).

College Trustees Play a Potent Role. New York: Council for Financial Aid to Education, Inc., 1957.

DAVIS, PAUL H. "If You Were a Trustee XXV," *Memo to the Board,* Series 8, 1959.

————. "More to be Valued are They Than Gold," *Association of American Colleges Bulletin,* XLIV (October 1958), pp. 391–398.

DEFFERRARI, ROY J. (ed.). *College Organization and Administration.* Proceedings of the Workshop on College Organization and Administration Conducted at the Catholic University of America, June 17–27, 1946. Washington, D.C.: Catholic University Press, 1947.

————. "The Problems of Administration in the American College," Proceedings of the Workshop on Problems of Administration in the American College Conducted at the Catholic University of America June 10–12, 1955. Washington, D.C.: Catholic University Press, 1956.

DIMOCH, MARSHALL E. *The Executive in Action* New York: Harper, 1945.

DUNCAN, ROBERT F. "College Trustees and the Raising of Money," A speech given March 24, 1960, at New York City College Seminar on Finance, by Kusting, Brown and Company, Inc., New York.

DURKEE, FRANK M. "Organizing for Growth in Service," *Educational Leadership,* 17:336–339 (Mar. 1, 1963), pp. 458–501.

GARDNER, JOHN W. Excellence, *Can We Be Equal and Excellent Too?* New York: Harper, 1961.

GONSER, THOMAS A. "How to Be A Successful College Trustee," *College and University Business* (July 1964), pp. 37–38.

HILL, ALFRED *The Small College Meets the Challenge.* New York: McGraw-Hill, 1959.

KEEZER, DEXTER M. (ed.). *Financing Higher Education: 1960–70,* New York: McGraw-Hill, 1959.

MARTORANA, S. V. *College Boards of Trustees*, Washington, D.C.: Center for Applied Research in Education, Inc., 1963.

MATHER, J. P. "Public Trusteeship: Pegasus or Dead Horse," *Association of Governing Boards Proceedings* (1956), pp. 38–48.

McVEY, FRANK L., and RAYMOND M. HUGHES. *Problems of College and University Administration*. Ames, Iowa: Iowa State College Press, 1952.

NIELSEN, OSWALD (ed.). *University Administration in Practice*. Stanford, Calif.: Stanford University Graduate School of Business, 1959.

PRAY, FRAN. "The New Trusteemanship," *College and University Journal*, Vol. 2, No. 2 (Spring 1963), pp. 9–16.

————. "The Trustees Mobilize for Development," paper presented at the Council for Financial Aid to Education, Inc., Trustees' Seminar, Beverly Hills, Calif., Nov. 22, 1963 (mimeo).

RUML, BEARDSLEY, and DONALD H. MORRISON. Memo to a College Trustee, *A Report on Financial and Structural Problems of the Liberal College*, New York: McGraw-Hill, 1959.

WEAVER, DAVID A. *Builders of American Universities*, Alton, Ill.: Shurtleff College Press, 1950.

WICKE, MYRON F. *Handbook for Trustees*, Division of Educational Institutions, Board of Education, The Methodist Church, Nashville, Tenn. Rev. ed., 1962.

WILSON, LOGAN. *The Academic Man, a Study in the Sociology of a Professor*. New York: Oxford U.P., 1942.

WIRT, ROBERT J. "What Are the New Developments in the Preparation of College Administrators?" in C. Kerry Smith (ed.), *Current Issues in Higher Education*. Washington, D.C.: Association for Higher Education, 1959.

CHAPTER 5

Communication

COMMUNICATING WITH THE BOARD OF TRUSTEES[1]

A student remarked recently at a major university, "Nobody really has any contact with the board of governors—it's like speaking to the gods on Olympus!"[2] In a survey of colleges and universities regarding communication with the board of trustees, it was found that few schools have any set policy on communication. It is important that college and university give some consideration to how that communication to their boards of trustees should take place.

In determining a policy for communicating with boards of trustees, the college and university administrators must first of all consider what objectives they wish to achieve. If the administrator wishes to control the institution in such a way as to allow the board to get only the information he wants them to get, he can rely upon a formal chain-of-command communication system. That is a system in which he stands between the board and all the other people within the institution. (See Figure 1.)

Most boards of trustees in the United States utilize the chain-of-command communication system in their organization. The major advantage of this is that it provides a method of filtering information to the board. If not reviewed, this information could be misinterpreted or cause great dissatisfaction at the board level. It basically prohibits "bad news" from getting to the board.

The control of information is centralized in the president, and the power of his office is strengthened both to the board and within the institution. The chief executive in this type of communication system becomes the major vehicle of power apart from the board of trustees. This power must be carefully executed lest it lead to a dictatorial approach by the president. Some institutions, however, may have personality characteristics that need such control vested in the individual.

A third advantage of the chain-of-command method is efficiency of

[1] Orley R. Herron and Harold Miller, "Who Should Talk To Your Board of Trustees," *College and University Business Journal*, Vol. 43, No. 3 (September 1967), pp. 6–12.
[2] "The Unknown Rulers," *Time*, Vol. 89 (May 12, 1967), p. 52.

FIGURE 1

CHAIN OF COMMAND COMMUNICATION SYSTEM

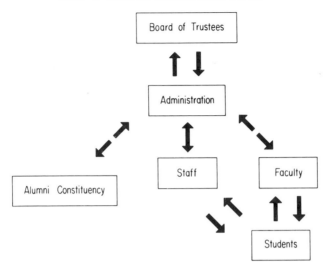

planning, because with it the agenda of the board meetings can be more rigidly programmed and structured. The president of the institution and the chairman of the board with the chain-of-command approach make certain that no information is placed on the agenda without their knowledge or approval. This method gives administrators adequate time to prepare for the meeting and discourages digressions.

Lastly, such a communication system will lessen the need for many board meetings. The board would deal only with major policy matters, and smaller policy decisions would be an administrative prerogative.

The main disadvantage to this method of communication is that it has a tendency to give board members "tunnel vision" regarding the college. The board's contacts with other agencies of the institution are limited and therefore the picture they receive is mainly the "good news upward" approach. The term "good news upward" was coined by Ralph Nichols, reporting on research studies of communication within industry.

He reported that workers understood less than 25 percent of what their managers thought they understood. In addition, management tended to give an optimistic estimate of the morale of the employees when in actuality employees did not feel that way. The main reason for this discrepancy, according to Nichols, was the supervisors' failure to report disturbing information upward to the management.[3] College administrators are tempted to do the same in reporting to a board.

[3] Ralph G. Nichols, Chairman of the Department of Rhetoric, University of Minnesota, unpublished manuscript, pp. 4–5.

Another disadvantage to the chain-of-command approach is that it can direct board members to deal mainly with pressing fiscal matters. This is quite natural, since a majority of board members are business oriented and their role as trustee requires considerable attention to business, development, and plant concerns.

Equally as important to this concern is the fact that a chain-of-command system can create policies that are approved by the board without participation of all agencies affected by the policy. Our research has also discovered that the academic aspects of the institution can take second place if not carefully guarded by the college and board communities. These policies appear to some academic communities as edicts, and do not receive their wholehearted support or recommendation. Robert Hess, former Minnesota regent, summarized this point when he stated that "university people simply aren't yes men."[4]

The final disadvantage of the chain-of-command method is that it tends to increase the "isolation gap" between the institution and the board. This isolation can create an attitude of misunderstanding within the institution which could have costly and demoralizing results.

If, on the other hand, the administrator wishes to involve the board in deeper interaction in the affairs of the college and to minimize the misunderstandings between the board and faculty, students and constituents, he can move to a dynamic communication system. That is, a system in which the board is central and all of the elements of the institution are represented to the board. (See Figure 2.)

FIGURE 2

DYNAMIC COMMUNICATION SYSTEM

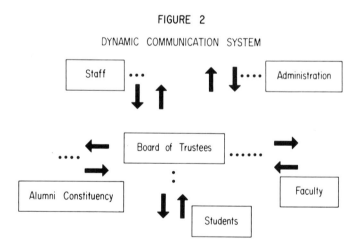

There are decided advantages to this approach. Chiefly, it enables us to solve the problem posed by a board that gets its information about the college only by memos devised and distributed by the president.

[4] "The Unknown Rulers," *op. cit.*

Under the new system the board will be more aware of the reality of the situation. Recently, the present author talked to the board chairman of a small junior college. There had been a faculty and student uprising over, among other things, academic freedom. The board chairman said: "As far as we knew, everything was rosy. But all the time we were sitting on a powder keg. When it went off, we weren't ready for it." The uprising cost the president his job. With the dynamic communication system, he would not have been held entirely responsible for misunderstanding the potential difficulty. The board members would have been placed more in the mainstream of information.

Another advantage of the dynamic system is the experience it gives to students and faculty in participating in decisions that are usually made by the administration and board alone. A classic study was undertaken by Coch and French on the use of discussion in instituting changes in production techniques in industry. Their findings showed that when employees have no voice in the planning of changes they resist those changes. On the other hand, when employees are given the right to set new standards for work, they are more apt to accept those standards as their own.[5]

A third advantage of a more dynamic system of communication is the broader understanding of the institution which it gives the board. Rather than attention to plant management and fiscal matters, the board's contacts with students and faculty members now help them to visualize the educational operation of the college in broader terms; students and faculty become something more than mere bodies filling rooms.

But while a dynamic system of communication has advantages, it takes a confident administrator to institute it. The chief danger in this approach to a board of governors is that the administrator relinquishes some of his right to control the operation of the institution. No longer can the president insulate the board from the facts of a given situation until he has worked out the solution. With open lines of communication from the students and faculty, there is little opportunity for the president to decide by himself what will be told and what will be withheld.

Perhaps a more practical problem in the dynamic communication system is the large amount of time which it takes. There can be no doubt that reports from the president, deans, and financial officers covering all facets of institutional operation at quarterly board meetings are simpler and less time-consuming than joint meetings of the board and the faculty, the students, the staff, and the alumni. Time usage is crucial; make sure it is used appropriately.

[5] Lester Coch and John R. P. French, Jr., "Overcoming Resistance to Change," in D. Cartwright and S. Zander (eds.), *Group Dynamics: Research and Theory*, New York: Harper, 1960, pp. 319–341.

POLICY ON COMMUNICATING WITH BOARDS OF TRUSTEES

Wisconsin's Regent Kenneth Greenquist stated that, "there is no balance sheet with a univeristy—you could make a mistake and not know it for a generation."[6] The prospect of a college careening along with little knowledge of the effects of its operation is a frightening one to the society which supports and nurtures it.

Of course, the trustee cannot know all there is to know about the operation of the university he serves, but the effectiveness of the institution depends in large measure, on his having timely and pertinent information—in other words, on some policy that gets feedback to the board quickly.

The author's feeling here is that an ideal policy for communication is a method which is a modification of both the chain-of-command approach and the dynamic approach. A method of this nature can be devised which incorporates the advantages of both systems. This gives full advantage of efficiency of operation, administrative control, faculty-student involvement in administration-board decisions, and minimizing the isolation gap. The author proposes a Modified Chain-of-Command System as a policy for communicating with boards of trustees. (See Figure 3.)

Efficiency of operation is essential to successful management. A chain of command affords this efficiency. The disadvantages of this basic

FIGURE 3

THE MODIFIED CHAIN-OF-COMMAND SYSTEM

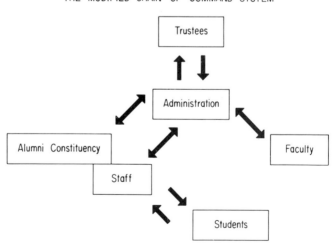

[6] "The Unknown Rulers," *op. cit.*

plan of organization, though significant, are not inherent in the structure. The need for increased trustee involvement in the affairs of the college or university can be met within this structure if it is given minor modifications.

In the first place, *the board should be organized into committees covering all phases of the college operation.* Most colleges and universities have already done this. Before the committees are formed, however, the board should define the needs of the institution. Once they are defined, the board can divide itself into the most appropriate committees to meet those needs. Generally speaking, the committees created can be: the executive committee (composed of the chairman of each committee plus the chairman of the board); the finance committee; the student services committee; the development and long-range planning committee; the education committee; the building committee; and the membership committee. These committees basically represent the major agencies within the institution. Most important is the fact that these committees can be the vehicle for maximum fluidity and centrality of communication.

A key modification which the author believes will increase the interaction between the board and the rest of the institution is the make-up of the committees. Each committee on the board should have carefully selected representative faculty, student, staff, and alumni persons serving where their presence would help the board in formulation of policies that will affect them. For example, the education committee could have (with a least ex-officio status), the dean of faculty, one or two faculty members, and student representatives. Since board members are often successful businessmen, they bring the assumptions of practical experience to deliberations on educational policies. This is a two-edged sword. The educational community needs some contacts with the "real world," but it needs an unusual amount of freedom and time for teaching and research to be most effective. Constant interaction between students, faculty, administrators, and the board in committee will help the board to understand more fully the educational operation of its institution, will help the faculty and students see the practical implications of policy decisions, and will aid the administrator in interpreting information both ways.

Another example of this plan would be the development long-range planning committee. Here certain alumni and veteran faculty members can help give the board a better understanding of the long-range picture. Recently, a faculty member of a major Midwestern university remarked to the author: "My university had one of the finest sociology departments in the world, and yet it made decisions which placed it in the midst of one of the worst big-city environments in the country." Long-range planning involving disintegrating neighborhoods and university environments should turn to its own faculty experts in architure and environmental planning for help in finding solutions.

These members could not only help boards to better understand the total operation of the college and to know some of the thinking of the people who are affected by those policies, but they also can help the administration interpret these policies and explain to their peers the reasoning that has gone into their deliberations. Thus a bridge has been built to span the isolation gap.

Since communication is essential for a successful operation of an institution, I recommend a policy that insures efficiency and incorporates open lines of communication. In the author's judgment, these goals can best he met by a modified chain-of-command system.

THE COMPASS OF HIGHER EDUCATION[7]

The agenda for the board of trustees meeting is one of the most powerful yet most neglected aspects of higher education. The agenda determines to a great extent the direction and future of an institution of higher learning. It also determines and defines how the board member will give his time, ability, and effort to his particular institution. Both of these determinants can limit or strengthen the educational growth of the board corporately and individually.

In my personal research concerning boards I have discovered that many board agendas are planned hurriedly, researched haphazardly, and expedited poorly. One must ascertain that the lack of preparation and adequate planning of board agendas could be the prologue to many troubled and difficult times of an institution. In extreme cases it could be the portent of the demise of a school.

Admittedly, the personality and educational makeup of a board varies from one institution to another. Therefore, boards will react differently to the same agenda.

It can be surmised, however, that efficient, thorough, and carefully planned agendas are characteristic of successful boards. Judicious and diligent programming has never been listed among the characteristics of institutions that failed.

If a board is to chart the destiny of an institution, the information brought before it must be of the highest excellence and validity. For it is within the board meeting that the most critical and influential decisions will be made.

I submit, therefore, five considerations that may strengthen a board meeting and thus the course of higher education.

[7] Orley R. Herron, "The Compass of Higher Education," *College and University Business Journal*, Vol. 63, No. 6 (December 1967).

First, always make sure there is adequate time to properly prepare an agenda for the board meeting. Remember, it is always better to enter an item for review at the next board meeting rather than to make a decision on that item without adequate facts. If one is not vigilant, a board can be conditioned to mediocrity by permitting decisions to be made without adequate information. If trustees were graded on their "homework" there would be some embarrassed faces.

Second, set definite guidelines to what information may be acted upon or considered at the board level. Many board meetings are preoccupied with small details that could have been easily expedited by a staff member. The agenda should be so structured that only major policy items are given priority at the board level. Some governing boards, however, are so incorporated that they must authorize even the smallest item of expenditure within the institution. Such picayunish authorization is not advantageous to the actualizing of the maximum excellence in an academic community. Delegation saturated in trust is a key to administration efficiency.

Third, distribute the agenda with the background information included prior to the actual meeting. All too regularly trustees get their first look at a board agenda after the meeting convenes. Few trustees can make reliable and valid judgments if they must synthesize all information for a decision with such faulty preparation. Every trustee member should receive information for a board meeting at least one week in advance, and even with that amount of time it is a gamble. Ideally, two to three weeks of preparation for a meeting are essential.

Fourth, permit resource individuals to be available at each board meeting if they can strengthen and clarify information being presented to the board. Some boards are structured so rigidly that only individuals defined by their corporate laws can be permitted to enter the board meetings. In most institutions, the president normally attends, but often he is either the lone barrier to or the vehicle for communication with the board. This is risky business unless the president is almost super-human. He cannot synthesize and communicate information accurately from every agency that is being considered within the institution. The top management team plus resource people should be nearby to solidify all presentations to the board.

Fifth, centralize the planning of the agenda. The president of the institution and the chairman of the governing board should be the main individuals preparing the agenda. Centralization of planning will permit greater efficiency and will discourage information being presented to the board without prior review. Power blocs can be created in the board if there is too much decentralization in planning and in expediting policy matters.

It cannot be overemphasized that the board meeting is a critical aspect of higher education and the board agenda its educational compass. Take a long and careful look at how you formulate, distribute, and expedite your board agendas. Oversight in this area should and must be eliminated.

REGULARITY OF BOARD MEETINGS

The full board should meet as regularly as once a month to permit wider participation of the board in trustee affairs. Few boards meet weekly, most meet quarterly or biannually. The average regularity of meeting is approximately six times a year. To meet less than four to six times is to risk invalidating the authority and power of the board. If the governing board is to understand the multifaceted undertakings of an institution, it needs to meet at least quarterly to maintain at best a nominal level of insight in an institution's operations. Even under normal conditions governing boards have difficulty performing their roles; diminishing or cutting off communication is almost equivalent to eliminating the board itself. A board should review annually its regularity of meetings and decide if a revision in scheduling is necessary. There is probably no ideal standard on the number of times a board to be successful should convene with its full membership. Each institution is unique and must analyze its programs and purposes to determine the requisite number of meetings. While there is a danger of too little communication, there is also danger of too much, which can degenerate into "meddling." Involvement in administrative prerogatives can usurp the power of the administration by interfering with their day-to-day internal affairs. This is certainly tantamount to undermining potentially strong and capable leadership. The board should allow the administrators to run the internal affairs of the institution. Communication requires knowledge, participation, and techniques—but never usurpation.

The executive committee of the board is an excellent committee, but a full board must be careful in not delegating too many responsibilities to it.

THE CHAIRMAN OF THE BOARD AND THE PRESIDENT

The chairman of the board and the president of the institution should meet regularly. Once a month can be a standard procedure which would permit excellent interaction to occur. These meetings can be convened at dinner, luncheon, or breakfast, or at an appropriate location that permits ease of communication. The president's office or the board chairman's office is a fine location if interruptions can be eliminated. The working relationship between the two heads can never be underestimated or overstated. It is the key to the smooth operation of institutions. Friction, lack of communication, or disrespect should never be characteristics of their relationship. A president must not "hide" derogatory or dissatisfactory information from the chairman. The confidence of their communication must be founded on high standards that insure the wisest discernment in the dissemination of their viewpoints and decisions. The president is the chief executive of the institution and the chairman his top adviser and confidant. Presidents that choose to communicate only irregularly with the chairman are missing many valuable opportunities for improvement. There may be some exceptions to this rule, however, because of mitigating circumstances.

The meetings should be individual meetings between only the two chiefs unless the nature of the communication requires assistance from delegated officers or trustees. If a president and board chairman meet fairly regularly, the chairman of the board should live in fairly close proximity to the institution—within a 100–300-mile radius. If a board chairman has his own private jet plane (some do) and sufficient means of transportation to get to the appropriate location, then greater distances are permissible.

This brings up the matter of expenses. The budgeting of the institution should include funds for the expense of board meetings. A president normally has a reasonable travel budget. Too few institutions, however, have set up travel funds for board meetings to underwrite the expenses of the trustees. All institutions should establish an account in their budget to pay for the travel expenses necessary to insure the attendance of trustees at their regularly convened meetings. Time is usually so valuable to a trustee anyway that his travel expense will not be a major recurring item or a large total in the annual budget. Institutions that pay the full expenses of the trustees for their meetings have higher attendance than those who do not. This should also include funds for the monthly meetings of the president and chairman of the board and other members who are necessary at the meeting.

The college can also provide adequate assistance in securing proper overnight accommodations and adequate transporation for the trustees during the meeting. The trustees usually require some help in getting motel or hotel space and taxi service (furnished by the institution) in getting to and from the meetings and elsewhere.

COMMITTEE CHAIRMEN

The president of the college should meet regularly with each chairman of the committees of the board. The president can meet individually as well as collectively with the committee chairmen. These meetings should be a time of strategy planning as well as depth analysis of the

tasks that each committee is assigned. It is essential that the president
provide each committee chairman with the staff, tools, and information
necessary for understanding of the task at hand. The committee chairmen are crucial in the effective functioning of the board and the time
spent with them will be extremely beneficial. Through these contacts the
president can give each member a more sophisticated veiw of his
respective roles and of the nature of the educational process. They will
gain a closer understanding of one another. The one-to-one contact is
still a highly effective technique of teaching and proper use of that meeting will be advantageous to the institution. Disagreement and misunderstandings can be explored, exposed, and eliminated in these one-to-
one meetings. The committee chairmen are the vital links with the chairman of the board in the efficient execution of the governing board's
responsibilities. The one-to-one meetings should be informal, direct, and
held at the most convenient location. Timing of the meetings must be
such that it is most appropriate in the scheduling of affairs for the institution's progress. This means that the committee chairman will deal only
with the most essential and necessary assignments, avoiding trivia and
items that are really not in the best interest of the time and attention.
The president should permit the board members "to get anything off
his chest" that could later present difficulty at the board level. The
president must be a specialist in creating the atmosphere where opinions
and honesty can prevail which breeds cohesion and strength.

BOARD MEMBERS AND FACULTY COMMUNICATION

A president will decide to what extent, if any, he wants board
members on their own initiative and volition to discuss with faculty directly any matters relating to the conduct of their professional duties.
If the college has a fairly loosely structured communication system, such
discussions could occur rather frequently. The president stands in the
gap to assist the board and faculty in contacts that could otherwise become inappropriate or detrimental to their institution. Direct contact may
bring understanding and support, but it also can generate suspicion, ill
feeling, and misunderstanding. Most faculty members feel that questioning of their conduct by a board member is an infringement and can lead
to a highly explosive situation. Faculty members do not welcome criticism of trustees relative to their teaching. A trustee must move cautiously
in such delicate matters, realizing that it is always wiser to act through
such delegated academic personnel as deans and similar liaison executive officers. On the other hand, a president should not discourage a
trustee from contacting a faculty member if his comments are to be
laudatory and commendable. A rule of thumb then would be that if a
board member wants to question or criticize the professional conduct of

a faculty member he should always go through a designated intermediary. If the trustee wants to praise a faculty member he might do so by letter or on an individual basis. A trustee can exert pressure upon a faculty member, and if the former insists upon talking directly to a faculty member, thereby ignoring the foregoing advice, the freedom of the institution is indeed threatened. The chairman of the board should intervene and advise the trustee that he is out of order and to desist. A president and dean may determine that it is advisable to convene a meeting between the trustee, the dean, and the faculty member in question to seek a valid understanding of the situation. This approach can be very embarrassing to a trustee as well as to the faculty, and may cause a traumatic situation that will not easily be forgotten. If, however, the nature of the communication system in one of openness, frankness, respect, then such communication may be deemed very appropriate.

BOARD MEMBERS AND ADMINISTRATOR CONTACTS

The president and chairman of the board should determine to what extent board members may contact administrators other than the president regarding their areas of responsibility. Here again the communication policy will determine the nature and frequency of contacts with administrators and board members. Some presidents have suffered battle scars when board members have contacted administrators and solicited information which in the final analysis is not complimentary to the president or institution. This type of contact should be stopped. Many a president has shuddered when questioned regarding a "tasty morsel" of information from obscure or unidentified sources. The atmosphere and environment must be so structured that any contact between board members and administrators is always founded upon the highest standards of ethics. Without question the administrator in charge of a specific area is likely to be the person most knowledgeable of the matters pertaining to that area. He therefore should be allowed to speak for his area but not for others outside his supervision. A college can function with freedom of board members and individual administrators' contacts when it can assist in the development of understanding and above all in the progress of the institution.

A president must never be envious of highly capable administrators who win the confidence of the board but should understand that strong administration with strong presidents breeds success.

NATURE OF BOARD-INSTITUTION CONTACTS

A president should decide within the scope and nature of his institution if he should encourage board members to contact any individual within the institution without his knowledge. Here again the decision will depend upon whatever written or unwritten type of communication policy is in existence at their institution. Strong arguments for and against such contact can be listed. The key to it all should be the understanding of the board relative to the process of higher education. If the board members have a fairly sophisticated grasp of the variegated vectors of higher education and all that these entail, then any contact within the institution should prove to be meaningful. Whether a board member contacts individuals apart from the president's knowledge will then be incidental. The president must encourage the board to obtain all the information it can about any areas of the college so long as the nature of contacts is in the best interests of the institution. The chairman of the board can advise board members that such contacts should never lead to favoritism or prejudicial viewpoints. Many boards of large colleges and universities have an understanding that any contacts with board members other than the president will be communicated to the president. The president of such institutions seldom discourages contacts as long as they are proper and necessary. Most board members will not have the time to develop contacts with individuals other than the president or other executive officers. Trustees find it extremely difficult to attend many of the scheduled full board meetings; "extra fringe meetings," such as with individual staff, or faculty members, may be highly improbable unless, of course, the board member is retired or has much time on his hands and desires these contacts. We will speak later about retired people serving on the board.

PATTERNS OF COMMUNICATION

Communicating with boards certainly involves other than personal meetings. The president should establish a pattern of communication that involves keeping the trustees posted on all the up-to-date news. The president can write a bimonthly letter to each individual board member giving him a digest and chronicle of items of primary interest. He can state his reaction and response to certain items that require additional information. This letter should not be mimeographed or multilithed but can be "Hoovenized," or typed on paper- or magnetic-tape electric typewriters that produce a number of originals simultaneously. Personal communication and attention is vital to a trustee, and the president should be a skilled professional at using it. The "coldness" of a mimeographed or multilithed letter can be offensive to individual board members and the president should eliminate the use of it in his letters to the board.

In addition to the one personal newsletter and the president's response to the most important events occurring on campus, other pieces of information should be mailed to the board. The student newspaper can also be included; this publication can be highly upsetting to the board if it is not properly understood. It is wise to send the board the student newspaper because the latter usually expresses some of the flavor of student opinion, evaluations, and feelings on the campus. Too much information that goes out to the board is deciphered, censored, and cut so that the board member may not ever see a true picture of what is really going on among the students. The student newspaper is one way of bridging the gap though the paper may create confrontations that need long explanation.

The public relations office, development office, intercollegiate department, and the alumni office will be printing brochures, newsletters, press releases. All of these can be mailed to the board, though many may not be read. Most important is that the academic and business affairs should be communicated to the board. They most likely will understand the business affairs and give excellent attention to them. The academic affairs should never be neglected in communication because of the board's proneness to business. The best approach to the board in these matters is to summarize what is transpiring; if details are requested then present them at length.

The development of the conference sessions via the telephone has proved to be highly successful for handling of some board business. However, it does not substitute for the personal interaction that is lost when there is no visual contact with the board members. The president and trustees may choose from time to time to hold committee meetings or discussion via a "live" conference telephone, and this should not be discouraged.

OPEN OR CLOSED BOARD MEETINGS

The Oregon State Board of Higher Education inaugurated a policy in 1967 whereby student viewpoints could be presented at first hand at its meetings. Student governments at each of the nine institutions in the Oregon State system of higher education agreed to help defray the expenses of a student to represent them at all meetings. The members of the board hear the student representative, along with the executive from the state's public college and universities who attend all board meetings. The invitation for a student spokesman at the meetings came the spring of 1967 when student efforts to forestall a tuition hike were unsuccessful. The student leaders complained at the time that they did not have an opportunity to make their case known until after the tuition increase had been approved. This opportunity for students to communicate firsthand at the board meetings is an excellent step in creating good will and understanding between the board and the institution. If it proves successful, such a policy should be adopted by the majority of boards of trustees.

The Rhode Island Board of Trustees of state colleges reversed its twenty-eight-year-old policy of holding only closed sessions, and has unanimously adopted (starting in the fall of 1967) the principle of open meetings. The closed-meeting policy was criticized "as more restrictive than any that came to our attention" by Paul L. Fisher, Director of the Freedom of Information Center at the University of Missouri. He made a nationwide survey of the open-or-closed meeting policies of the governing boards of state colleges and universities.[8] The Rhode Island decision was announced after a closed meeting. The first open meeting occurred in October, 1967. The procedure of the open meeting is as follows:

Meetings to be Open

Meetings of the Board shall be open and accessible to the public, subject to limitations of space and to such reasonable restrictions as shall be imposed by the Chairman or by vote of the Board in particular situations to assure the orderly conduct of business; provided, however, that disciplinary, personnel, and confidential matters the disclosure or public discussion of which would, in the opinion of a majority of the members present, be unduly detrimental to the individuals involved or to the effective discharge of the Board's responsibilities, may be discussed in executive session.

Minutes of Meetings

Minutes of open meetings shall be deemed public records. Minutes of executive sessions shall be confidential, but final action taken in executive session shall be reported by the Chairman at the next open meeting of the Board and shall be recorded as part of the minutes of such open meeting.

Press and Public Relations

The Chancellor and the chairman are authorized to release the agenda of open meetings to news media prior to the meeting on condition that no material included therein, other than the identity of the topics to be considered at the meeting, shall be published or broadcast prior to the meeting. The Chairman shall be the chief spokesman for the Board and the members shall, to the extent possible and consistent with the proper discharge of their individual responsibilities, refer all inquiries which concern interpretation of Board action and policy to the Chairman. The Chancellor is authorized to answer all

[8] Published by Freedom of Information Center (Paul Fisher), "Access to Records and Governing Boards of Tax-Supported Universities" (University of Missouri, February 1965, Position Paper N), pp. 1–4.

inquiries concerning the office of the Chancellor and any questions of fact concerning the Board or its actions on other than confidential matters.[9]

Once this policy is adopted, it will no longer be necessary for the Board to hold press conferences the day following the regularly scheduled meetings, and this practice will be abandoned.

Notices of the regular meetings will not be sent to the news media, since it is established that regular meetings are held on the first Wednesday of every month except the month of August. The place of the meeting alternates between the University of Rhode Island and Rhode Island College. The October 4, 1967, meeting was held in the Senate Chamber of the Memorial Student Union at the University of Rhode Island. The November meeting was to be held at Rhode Island College; and unless notified, the meetings alternate regularly. All meetings convene at 9:30 A.M.

The news media will be notified if special meetings of the Board are convened. This does not apply to Executive Sessions.

The press and public will attend these meetings as observers. Under no circumstances will they be invited to participate.

Agenda of the meetings will be posted at the door of the meeting room. Any news media wishing to see the agenda in advance of the meeting may do so by requesting this information directly from the Board of Trustees Office, 199 Promenade Street, Providence, R. I. The agenda will be available two working days before the regularly scheduled meeting. Requests for agenda will be honored; however, occasionally items are not placed on the agenda in time to notify the news media in advance.

At every regular meeting of the Board, members of the Public Relations Departments of the University of Rhode Island and Rhode Island College will be present to assist news media. The Public Relations Departments will continue the practice of sending releases of background material on those items they consider newsworthy. Any special requests for background material will be received by the Public Relations offices at the University of Rhode Island and Rhode Island College and at Rhode Island Junior College.[10] They are to make arrangements through the public relations office of the institution where the meeting is to be held if they wish to use cameras, TV equipment, or audio equipment.

The degree and style of open board meetings is likely to come under considerable discussion in the months and years ahead. Newsmen as well as some citizens are particularly anxious to be present during the discussion of board meetings. The argument for closed meetings to the public is to guarantee confidence in matters that need not be disclosed to the public. Many a governing board or administrator has been stung by misinterpretations of facts or unwarranted criticism of actions of the governing board. In 1960 Victor J. Dailos, director of the Univer-

[9] Board of Trustees of State Colleges, "Open Meetings of the Board of Trustees" (Sept. 29, 1967), Providence, Rhode Island, pp. 1–2.
[10] *Ibid.*

sity of Colorado, learned from 67 of 93 tax-supported institutions returning his questionnaire that governing boards meetings of three out of
four were open some of the time. Paul Fisher found that the governing
boards of the Universities of Minnesota, Wisconsin, Michigan, and Nebraska rank among those that have made liberal concessions to press
coverage. The University of Colorado regents meetings are open but
the executive sessions are allowed on request of the University president or two regents. Minnesota has provided for "seminars" during which
personnel is discussed. The University of California board of regents
meetings are open though certain sensitive matters . . . identified in the
board's bylaws—may be closed and acted upon in closed sessions.[11]

"Paul Fisher has discovered that there is some complication in the
states with open-meeting statutes which vary in detail while maintaining a general similarity." His center indicated that these statutes take
little power from the boards that are directly referred to only in
Oklahoma, Nevada, and Utah laws. Executive sessions of public bodies
are permitted under all the states, though some states define the conditions under which they may be called. These conditions might be the
discussion of personnel, discussion of financial matters where publicity
might cause loss to the state, or hearings of witnesses in matters under
investigation by public agencies. The Freedom of Information Center
also determined that the range of these provisions for survey would appear to cover the requirements of the boards. It is considerably greater
than that given to boards in Oklahoma, where the discussions of individuals may be closed, or in Nevada, where financial discussion must be
kept open.

The Center indicates that open-meetings statutes are unanimous in
providing that final acts cannot be taken except in open meetings. A
Wisconsin State attorney general's opinion holding that the Wisconsin
open-meeting *law* extends to faculty committee meetings may be the only
known example of its kind.

The relevancy of open-record statutes has revealed that most states
have open-record status. They apparently make numerous and varied
exceptions to disclosure and commonly exclude from inspection those
records closed by the statutes. Among statutes bearing on our point here
are those empowering the governing boards to create such bylaws, ordinances, regulations, and rules as are necessary and expedient to the discharge of the duties of the board or in the best interests of the institution. Reasonable interpretation would indicate that this power extends
to closing the records of the university or colleges where this is found
to be in the best interest as determined by the board of the institution.[12]

---

[11] Board of Trustees of State Colleges, *loc. cit.*
[12] *Ibid.*

CHECKLIST FOR BOARD COMMUNICATION

A checklist that a president can use for analyzing his board relative to communication is as follows:

1. Who plans the agenda for your board meetings?
2. Please state as simply as you can what kinds of information presented at the board meetings regarding the college and its program cause the greatest amount of satisfaction by the board.
3. Please state as simply as you can what kinds of information presented at the board meetings regarding the college and its program cause the greatest amount of dissatisfaction by the board.
4. How often does the full board of trustees meet? _____Weekly _____Monthly _____Quarterly _____Semiannually _____ Annually _____Other
5. What members of the administration other than the president meet regularly with the board at these meetings?
6. Please indicate to what extent you meet individually with trustees between regular board meetings? _____Regularly _____ Quite frequently _____Sometimes _____Infrequently _____ Not at all
7. Please indicate to what extent you meet individually with the chairman of the board. _____Regularly _____Quite frequently _____Sometimes _____Infrequently _____Not at all
8. Is your board organized on the committee basis? Yes_____ No_____
9. Please indicate which committees have been formed. Building _____ Development_____ Education_____ Student_____ Personnel_____ Financial_____ Other_____
10. Please indicate to what extent you meet with these committees. Regularly_____ Quite frequently_____ Sometimes_____ Frequently_____ Not at all_____
11. Please indicate to what extent you meet individually with the committee chairman. Regularly_____ Quite frequently_____ Sometimes_____ Infrequently _____ Not at all_____
12. Please indicate to what extent board members visit campus on their own to converse with students.
13. Please indicate to what extent board members on their own contact faculty directly regarding conduct of their professional duty. _____Regularly _____Quite frequently _____Sometimes _____Infrequently _____Not at all
14. Please indicate to what extent board members on their own contact administrators other than the president regarding their areas of responsibility. _____Regularly _____Quite frequently _____ Sometimes _____Infrequently _____Not at all
15. Do you as president encourage board members to contact individuals in the institution without your knowledge? Yes_____ No_____
16. Do you have a written policy regarding communication between board members and individuals within the institution? Yes _____ No_____ (If yes, please indicate.)

Some of these questions were sent to presidents of 90 college and universities. Fifty-seven responses were usable and the responses were shown in Table 1 through Table 7.

TABLE 1

Frequency of Full Board Meetings in Accredited and Nonaccredited Institutions

Frequency of Meetings	All Institutions	
	Number	Percentage
Weekly	—	—
Monthly	1	1.7
Quarterly	16	28.1
Semi-annually	27	47.4
Annually	5	8.8
Other	6	10:5
No response	2	3.5
Total	57	100.0

TABLE 2

Regularity of President's Meeting with Committees of the Board

Regularity	All Institutions	
	Number	Percentage
Regularly	17	29.8
Quite frequently	12	21.0
Sometimes	11	19.4
Infrequently	5	8.8
Not at all	—	—
No response	12	21.0
Total	57	100.0

TABLE 3

Regularity of President's Meeting with Chairman of the Board

Regularity	All Institutions	
	Number	Percentage
Regularly	14	24.6
Quite frequently	23	40.3
Sometimes	16	28.1
Infrequently	1	1.7
Not at all	—	—
No response	3	5.3
Total	57	100.0

TABLE 4

Regularity of President's Meeting with Individual Chairmen of Board Committees

Regularity	All Institutions	
	Number	Percentage
Regularly	3	5.3
Quite frequently	15	26.3
Sometimes	23	40.4
Not at all	6	10.5
No response	10	17.5
Total	57	100.0

TABLE 5

Regularity of President Meeting with Individual Board Members

Regularity	All Institutions	
	Number	Percentage
Regularly	12	21.0
Quite frequently	23	40.4
Sometimes	18	31.6
Infrequently	2	3.5
Not at all	2	3.5
Total	57	100.0

TABLE 6

Regularity of Board Members Contacting Faculty Directly Regarding Conduct of Their Professional Duty

Regularity	All Institutions	
	Number	Percentage
Regularly	—	—
Quite frequently	2	3.5
Sometimes	8	14.0
Infrequently	23	40.4
Not at all	21	36.8
No response	3	5.3
Total	57	100.0

TABLE 7

Regularity That Board Members on Their Own Contact Administrators Other Than the President Regarding Their Areas of Responsibility

Regularity	All Institutions	
	Number	Percentage
Regularly	—	—
Quite frequently	8	14.0
Sometimes	20	35.1
Infrequently	25	43.8
Not at all	3	5.3
No response	1	1.8
Total	57	100.0

An analysis of 1,100 trustees' responses to questions regarding information that engendered the greatest satisfaction by board members indicated that the following information in order of priority was the most satisfying.

1. Sound finances
2. Academic excellence
3. Physical expansion and development
4. Enrollment growth
5. Satisfaction of faculty
6. The tone of the institution and its cultural program
7. Public acceptance of policy
8. Satisfaction of staff

On the other hand, the information that caused the greatest amount of dissatisfaction to board members could be ranked in the following order.

1. Deficit financing
2. Details that take too much time
3. Faculty problems
4. Unhappy students
5. Poor business procedures
6. Staff incompetence
7. Admission decrease
8. Poor public relations

SUMMARY

There are various systems of communication. Two of these systems are the *chain-of-command* system and the *dynamic* system. Several advantages and disadvantages of both systems are worth mentioning. Chiefly, the advantages of the formal system (administrator reporting and interpreting happenings at the college to the board in formal meetings) are: (1) It encourages efficiency of planning operation of meetings, and (2) it tightens administrative control of reported information. The disadvantages of this approach are: (1) It limits trustees' understanding of the college to the administrator's view, (2) it lessens the likelihood of full appreciation of academic affairs of the institution, (3) it allows for little participation in policy-making by faculty, students, and others affected by those policies, and (4) it increases the isolation gap between the board and the institution.

The advantages of the dynamic approach (a system which puts the board in direct contact with all phases of the college operation) are: (1)

It places the board in a better position to understand the total operation of the college, (2) it allows the people who will be affected by the policy to help develop these policies, and (3) it helps the board to see the institution as it exists rather than through the eyes of one or a few persons. The disadvantages of this system are: (1) It causes the administrator to lose some control of the information which reaches the board, and (2) it consumes a great deal of time for the trustees to deal with the non-policy matters which would reach him in his relationship.

What is needed, then, is a system that provides a maximum of trustee involvement and efficiency. It seems that some modification of both the above-mentioned systems would provide the optimum policy of communication with boards of trustees. Therefore, the author proposes a modified chain of command as a policy for communicating with boards of trustees.

The agenda for the board of trustees meeting is one of the most powerful yet neglected aspects in higher education. Many board agendas are planned hurriedly, researched haphazardly, and expedited poorly.

The president must communicate regularly with his board chairman and committee chairmen. Their method of communication is vital to the college. A checklist can be devised to explore adequately the area of communication with the board.

QUESTIONS

1. What type of communication policy would be ideal for a governing board and college communication?
2. Who should plan the agenda for a board meeting? When should it be planned?
3. Are open board meetings the most successful method to suggest in today's society? Why or why not?
4. Describe the ways the president must communicate with the board.
5. Indicate the reasons for the regularity of communication between the president of the college and the board chairman.
6. How often should a president meet with committee chairmen, and why?

BIBLIOGRAPHY

ADAMS, A. S. "Relations Between Governing Boards and Administrative Officers," *Proceedings of the Association of Governing Boards of State Universities*, 1952, pp. 51–57.

BURNS, G. *Administrators in Higher Education*, Chapter 5: "Boards of Trustees and Regents," New York: Harper, 1962.

DAVIS, PAUL H. "The World Stands Aside," *Association of American Colleges Bulletin*, Vol. 43, No. 2 (1957), pp. 269–273.

LEWIS, WILMARTH. "The Trustees and the University," *Harvard Alumni Bulletin*, July 2, 1952.

LLOYD, GLEN A. "A Trustee Looks at His Job," *Liberal Education*, Vol. 45, No. 49 (December 1959), p. 500.

MOOS, MALCOLM, and FRANCIS E. ROURKE. *The Campus and the State*. Baltimore, Md.: John Hopkins Press, 1959.

MORRILL, JAMES L. *The Ongoing State University*, Minneapolis, Minn.: U. of Minnesota Press, 1960.

SIMON, HERBERT W. *Administrative Behavior*. New York: Macmillan, 1957.

STANFORD, E. V. "Functional Board of Trustees for the Catholic College," *Catholic Education Review*, LIX (February 1961), pp. 102–107.

CHAPTER 6

Case Studies of In-Service Education

Trustees need to be improved and upgraded. Clark Kerr has said that "trustees are in a terrible bind now unless they have a background in the education field or lengthy preparation by committee service." Their understanding is vital, because the university is one of the central institutions of society and thus vulnerable to attack.

There are institutions seeking to upgrade their trustees and in doing so have embarked on some remarkable programs of in-service education. This chapter includes an analysis of in-service education in seven selected private institutions.

The seven institutions selected were chosen for visitation and investigation because: (1) their in-service programs were functioning with some degree of success; (2) the president expressed a willingness to cooperate with the visit and the depth analysis; and (3) schools selected provided diversification of geographical location, the type of institutional control, and the nature of the institution's program.

Arrangements for the personal interviews were made with the presidents by both letter and telephone. The letter stated the purpose of the visitation and the telephone call verified the intention and the time of the appointment.

A brief description of the general nature of the college is presented with a detailed analysis of its board of trustees and its in-service education program.

Previous researchers found that the nature of an interview could be hazardous unless the interview structure permitted the respondent to answer basically the same questions. An interview sheet was devised to allow a similarity in the pattern of the inquiry. The following items were included in that guide sheet:

1. Basic institutional data
   (a) Enrollment.
   (b) Composition of the student body.
   (c) General nature and purpose of the college.

2. General administration and board data
   (a) Number, qualifications, and manner of selection of the board members.
   (b) Role of the board in policy formulation.
   (c) Nature of the board control and delegation of responsibilities.
   (d) Evaluation of strengths and weaknesses of the board.
   (e) Professional background including education of the board membership.
   (f) Evaluation of the board relative to educational perception.
   (g) Length of service of president. Method of selection.
   (h) Education, background, and qualifications of the president.
3. In-service education program
   (a) The role of the president in the in-service education program.
   (b) The role of the administration and faculty in the in-service education program.
   (c) The role of the chairman of the board, the role of the committee chairmen, the role of individual board members in the in-service education program.
   (d) The role of outside resource people in the in-service education program.
   (e) What activities or materials are involved in the in-service education program? Briefly describe the activities and materials utilized.
   (f) Is there a budget for in-service education? If response is affirmative, how is this budget determined?
   (g) What significant changes, if any, have been evidenced in the board as a result of the in-service education program?
   (h) What effect has the in-service education program had upon the strengths and weaknesses of the board?
   (i) Who is basically responsible for the overall supervision of of the in-service education program?
   (j) Why have the factors listed helped in the success of the in-service education program? Other factors?
   (k) Why have the factors listed hindered the success of the in-service education program? Other factors?
   (l) Briefly describe the in-service orientation program for new members.
   (m) What are the future plans for in-service education?
   (n) Additional information on selected questionnaire items was requested.
   (o) Additional information pertaining to the general understanding of the in-service education program was requested.

The major emphasis of the interview centered upon item 3 on the interview sheet. This was in keeping with the chief purpose of the visitation, which was the acquisition of a more comprehensive understanding of the total in-service education program. The interviewer sought to maintain a parallel assimilation in the pattern of questioning. However, the uniqueness of each program arranged to some extent the style of the interview. The investigator took handwritten notes during the interview and requested any materials that would explain more concretely the program being given to the researcher. Among the materials released were confidential papers that were acquired on a loan basis.

INSTITUTION A

Institution A is a fully accredited, independent college located in a suburban community of a swiftly growing western city. The enrollment is fewer than 2,500 students, most of whom reside in the college's own residence facilities. One-half of the students are enrolled from the state in which the college exists and the remaining students come from 35 states and 12 foreign countries.

The college offers 17 majors and one-third of the students are enrolled in an educational major. No graduate work beyond the fifth year educational requirement is offered.

Board of Trustees Organization

The board of trustees consists of 14 members with provision for membership of a total of 15 members. Ten executives, 1 clergyman, 1 lawyer, 1 medical physician, and 1 educator are the occupations represented on the board. Included in these occupations are 1 alumnus and 1 woman. Five trustees live within 100 miles of the college, 8 live from 100 to 500 miles away, and 1 member resides over 1,000 miles from the college. Two members are between the ages of 30 and 40, 6 members between the ages of 40 and 50, 4 between the ages of 50 and 60, and 2 over 60 years of age. Six members have earned a bachelor's degree, 2 have earned doctorates, 2 have been granted honorary degrees, and 4 members have not completed undergraduate school. The board is organized into 5 committees: (1) the building committee; (2) the development committee; (3) the education committee; (4) the financial committee; and (5) the membership committee. The chairman of each committee together with the chairman of the board compose the executive committee of the trustees. The board is a self-perpetuating corporation. The president has served in his office 15 years and accepted the presidential responsibilities from a background as a teacher and academic dean. Ten new members have been elected to the board while the president has served as chief executive. The occupations represented in this new membership are 7 executives, 1 lawyer, 1 medical physician, and 1 educator. The president, the dean of the faculty, and the business manager were interviewed during a two-day visit.

In-Service Education Program

Pre-School Workshop. Prior to the beginning of the fall semester a two-day faculty-trustee workshop is held apart from the campus so that the procedures affecting the workshop can be conducted without interruption. Formal and informal activities provide close interaction between the faculty and the trustees. Printed materials, lectures, panels, and slides are types of presentations used to assist in creating a clearer understanding of the nature of the activities of the college. One of the board members is the keynote speaker of the workshop, and the president normally terminates the two-day affair by a closing address. A professional educator from one of the neighboring large universities is invited to deliver at least one major speech relative to the role of faculty and the trustee in higher education. Excellent discussion usually follows each presentation and activity. A faculty-administrative committee plans the workshop and makes appropriate arrangements so that most participants can have overnight accommodations. A written evaluation is submitted by all persons involved in the workshop at the conclusion of its activities.

Annual Retreat. Annually the board of trustees conducts a weekend retreat designed to (1) help them understand their role; (2) plan activities and goals for the future; (3) develop a closer fellowship and appreciation of each other; (4) upgrade their understanding of higher education in general. This retreat, which is conducted in the second semester, is an excellent follow up to the faculty-trustee preschool workshop. Professional educators not affiliated with the college are invited to be the main speakers. These speakers have usually achieved national recognition in the area they represent. One member of the administration, the president, is invited to participate in all of the affairs of the retreat. Other administrators are encouraged to attend various phases of the weekend activities as they affect their individual responsibilities. A written or verbal evaluation is requested at the conclusion of the retreat.

Annual Board Meeting. Once a year the board meets to review the year that has just been completed. Normally the meeting is convened in the second month of the fall semester. Each administrator appointed to a board committee is invited to deliver a report on the activities affecting this commitee. These reports are part of the in-service education program and are geared to achieve the following: (1) to present a broader scope of the variegated aspects affecting the institution they serve; (2) to acclimate the board to the recent research relative to the techniques and methodology employed in their particular areas; (3) to allow direct communication between administration and the full board. An oral and written presentation is given and discussion is permitted following the individual presentations.

Trustee-Faculty Dinner. The evening prior to the annual meeting a trustee-faculty dinner is held on the college campus. The purpose of this dinner is to permit closer fellowship and interaction between the faculty members and their wives on the one hand and the board members and their wives on the other. Immediately following this dinner an informal program is presented by the student body. This type of student, faculty, and trustee interaction has increased the understanding and appreciation of one another's role.

Biweekly Mailings. The president prepares biweekly mailings to individual board members. Included in the mailings are these topics: (1) financial position of the college; (2) cultural and social activities of campus; (3) research conducted by the faculty; (4) professional meetings attended by the college staff; (5) plant development; (6) fund-raising program; (7) academic, physical, and spiritual concern of campus; (8) enrollment reports; (9) financial aid reports; (10) professional activities, and (11) books concerning the nature of higher education and trustees' role.

The mailings are intended to keep the trustees fully informed of all of the activities of the college and upgrade their understanding of them.

Attendance at Professional Meetings. Approximately once a year seminars are conducted by regional or national associations, which are patterned to assist the trustee in becoming more effective as a college board member. The president makes a strong effort to attract a sufficient number of trustees to attend these meetings. Reports and discussion of these meetings are given to the members who are unable to attend.

Monthly Meetings of the Executive Committee of the Board. The executive committee is composed basically of members who live within 100 miles of the college and are chairmen of board committees. A central location within a short driving distance from the college is maintained so that meetings can be more centralized. The monthly meetings are conducted in such a manner that (1) techniques of leadership are reviewed so that the chairman can motivate each individual committee member more properly; (2) topics discussed are fashioned to upgrade the understanding of the chairman relative to his committee responsibility; and (3) the nature, scope, and details of the college activities are discussed in depth.

Personal Conferences. Periodic conferences are held with individual members on a fairly regular basis. These conferences take the form of dinners; weekend visits in a trustee or the president's home; office calls; campus visitations to attend social, cultural, or athletic events; case studies and analysis; and travel guests of the president on trips concerning college business. The president attempts to analyze weaknesses and strengths of the trustees and address the conferences to them.

Special Consultants. Designated areas that evidenced limitations of personnel and knowledge sometimes necessitate the services of consultants. The area which has employed the use of a consultant most often has been that of development. Development counsel has been secured on a semester basis to widen the horizon of knowledge in the techniques of programming for development and also to determine successful methods of fund raising for the college staff.

Trustees as Speakers for the College to Outside Groups. A very efficient means of improving the trustee's understanding of the college was to utilize the trustee to speak to selected groups concerning the nature of the college. Preparation for the speeches deemed it necessary on occasion to read printed materials of the college, interview faculty and administration, review specified activities in professional education journals, analyze research-oriented books, and be acquainted with other current literature pertinent to the topic to be addressed.

Quarterly Full Board Meeting. The agenda is planned for the quarterly meetings in consultation with the executive council of the college, the executive committee of the board, and the chairman of the board. Although much of the agenda is dominated by legal or business affairs, each meeting focuses upon one aspect of the college that need to have a greater breadth of understanding by the board. Research personnel from the faculty, staff, administration, and outside are invited to assist the board achieve a more comprehensive analysis of the topic discussed.

Strengths and Weaknesses of the Program

The major weaknesses of the program were found to be lack of adequate follow-up to the programs, excessive volume of printed material given to the board, lack of time, and unavailability of some of the members to attend specialized meetings.

Summary of Institution A

The in-service education program for the board of trustees in Institution A is by its nature a combination of centralized and decentralized structure. The president assumes the main responsibility for the determination and supervision of the in-service education program. His immediate administrative staff assists in designing activities to improve the board understanding relative to their specific areas of responsibility. The chairman of the board and the chairmen of the committees of the board also assist in planning activities and procedures for trustee growth. The combination of both groups facilitating programs fashions the structure into a centralized and decentralized nature.

The president provides the impetus and inspiration to all participants in the improvement program and also provides standards to attain higher levels of personal educational growth.

The only budget for the program is expended for the special consultants and the speakers involved in the program. Very little expenditure is made for personal trustee expenses. The trustee is required to bear his own expenses for most of the in-service education activities.

Eleven phases constitute the in-service education program: (1) preschool workshop; (2) annual retreat; (3) annual board meeting; (4) trustee-faculty dinner; (5) biweekly mailings; (6) attendance at professional meetings; (7) monthly meetings of the executive committee of the board; (8) personal conferences; (9) special consultants; (10) trustees as speakers for college to outside groups; and (11) quarterly full board meetings.

The preschool faculty workshop and the annual retreat were acknowledged to be the most effective activities employed in the program. The excellent speakers invited to these meetings and the secluded location in which they were held contributed to the success of these activities.

The major weaknesses of the improvement program centered upon (1) lack of follow-up to the program; (2) too much printed material dispersed to the board; and (3) lack of time and availability of some of the board to attend meetings.

INSTITUTION B

Basic Institutional Data

Institution B is a private, fully accredited, church-related college located in a rural midwestern town. The enrollment is fewer than 2,000 students, of whom many reside in college-owned facilities. Seventy percent of the students are residents of the state in which the college exists and the remaining come from 15 states with few foreign students represented. Although the college is church controlled and affiliated, only 60 percent of the students are drawn from the church denomination the college serves. Twenty-four diversified religious denominations make up the religious composition of the student body.

The college was until recently a junior college offering general requirements in preparation of the final two years at another institution. With the expansion into a four-year program, additional courses have been added to allow for approximately twelve areas of specialization.

Board of Trustees Organization

The board of trustees consists of 24 members who are elected by the church conference, alumni, and the board itself. Nine financiers; 6 executives; 5 clergymen; 3 educators; and 1 medical physician compose the occupation diversification represented on the board. Twenty-two trustees live within 100 miles of the college and the remaining 2 live within 500 miles.

Three board members are between the ages of 30 and 40 years; 13 are between the ages of 40 and 50 years; 6 are between the ages of 60 and 70 years. No trustee is under the age of 30. Nine trustees have earned the bachelor's degree; 6 the master's degree; 1 the doctorate, who is the medical physician; and 6 had not completed college degree programs. Not one of the professional educators represented on the board has completed his doctorate studies.

The board is organized into 5 committees consisting of the building committee; the financial committee; the development committee; the education committee; and the student personnel committee. The president has been chief executive three years, having formerly been academic dean of the college he now serves. Six members have been elected to the board since he assumed the presidential role and they represent 2 executives; 2 financiers; 1 clergyman; and 1 educator. The president was interviewed during a one-day visit.

In-Service Education Program

New Member Orientation. Every new member elected to the board received an orientation speech delivered personally by the president of the college. The speech addresses itself to the goals of the college to which the member has been elected to serve. A one-day seminar is held at the church annual conference to orient the board member elected from the church constituency. All administrators take part in the seminar with each administrator presenting a 15-minute talk concerning his role and his individual responsibility at the college. Each new member is given an honorary seat in the executive committee of the board and is permitted to remain a part of that committee for a set period of orientation. The length of time a new member will serve on an honorary basis is determined by the board. The new members are invited to campus for one day to visit classes while they are in session. The teacher is aware of these visitations and the expectant frequency of them.

Periodic Mailings. The president sends mailings on a periodic basis to keep trustees aware of (1) their individual roles, (2) research undertaken by college staff, (3) the development and the plant program, and (4) the agenda of the committee meetings.

The book, *Memo to a College Trustee*, by Morrison and Ruml, is given to every member and is cited numerous times in the mailings. While the college was engaged in a self-study, prior to accreditation, constant communication and trustee involvement improved the trustee ability immensely. The basis for some mailings still have their origin in the self-study research.

Monthly Meetings. An advisory committee of the board meets monthly with the president. Previous presidents had encountered difficulty with the board regarding communication. The new president initiated the monthly meetings to assist the board in becoming more aware and adept in reference to college activities and procedures. These monthly meetings have proven highly successful. In addition, periodic meetings are convened with the executive board, which develops guidelines for the furtherance of board growth.

Trustee Research and Self-Study. A substantial grant by a large foundation provided the means by which the trustees could undertake an analysis of their own board. The self-study of their corporate structure has brought about many significant changes in policies and procedures affecting their academic decision-making processes, qualifications for membership, methods of election, occupational representation, and understanding of the trustee role, while also giving greater motivation for trustee participation in areas that need their strong support.

Trustees as Speakers to Church Conferences. Prior to the in-service education program the ministers of the college church denomination were commissioned to interpret the college at the conference meetings of the church delegates. After the inauguration of the improvement program, the trustees were selected to represent the college at all the major regional meetings of the conferences. Any discussion of the college at the conferences is now usually preceded by a lecture presented by one of the college trustees. The responsibility and preparation of the speeches have given the board members deeper insight into the forces that influence higher education and into their role at the college they serve. The penetrating questions that follow the address demand that the speaker be thoroughly cognizant of the college activities and procedures.

Trustee Chapels. Daily chapel services are held during each semester of the college. Trustees are invited to speak periodically in the chapel services. The opportunity to speak in these chapels affords the trustee more frequent contacts on campus visitations. Efficient preparation is made to provide the trustee the maximum potential for utilization of his time while on campus. These chapels permit personal informal conferences with members of the college academic community. The confrontation with various individuals of the college has increased the trustee awareness of the campus environmental climate.

Activities of the Board Committees. The inception of the in-service education program motivated the five board committees to become more effectively enlisted into the affairs of their committees. Prior to the in-service program the committees functioned more as honorary committees rather than active, working enthusiasts. The excellent results of their work are clearly evident in the progress made in many phases of the college program. A few of the improvements are: (1) expansion of the academic curriculum; (2) more adequate faculty salaries and long-range projection; (3) full accreditation; (4) increase in the physical and plant development; (5) attraction of more highly trained faculty and staff; (6) wider state and national attention; and (7) articles in professional journals commending work of the college.

Trustee-Faculty Dinner. Normally once a year and usually prior to the annual meeting a faculty-trustee banquet is held. The banquet has a threefold purpose: (1) bringing controlling agents of college into closer contact with college staff on a social basis; (2) commending participants on efforts in behalf of college; and (3) becoming better acquainted with the new members of the college staff and the board of trustees.

Class Visitations. On infrequent occasions the board members are invited to attend classes while in session. Although this is one of the phases of the orientation program for new members, all members are encouraged to attend class lectures or labs on periodic campus visits. The class visitations have been very satisfactory to the faculty and trustees. The president states that some of the invisible barriers that typically occur between board and faculty are slowly being torn down by the class visits. Most of the faculty do not consider they are on trial or being evaluated during the visits.

Consultants. Development consultants have been obtained to assist the board members in the campaign for additional funds for the college. Case-study analysis is conducted to help them more adequately understand their roles in the fund-raising program. Development counsel is employed on a compaign basis.

Strengths and Weaknesses of the Program

The new member-orientation program has become remarkably effective and is deemed to be one of the major strengths of the in-service education program. The periodic mailings have proven to be the most systematic tool employed in strengthening the board in academic and general knowledge concerning college affairs. Lack of time and the travel involved in attending campus meetings have hindered most the success of the program.

Summary of Institution B

The nature of the church relation of the college makes the in-service education program both centralized and decentralized. Some activities must be conducted on a regional basis without any major aspects of centralization.

The president plans and supervises the improvement program in consultation with his administrative staff and executive committee of the board. Ten phases compose the phases of the in-service program: (1) new-member orientation, (2) periodic mailings, (3) monthly meetings, (4) trustee research and self-study, (5) trustees as representatives to church conferences, (6) trustee chapels, (7) active board committees, (8) faculty-trustee dinner, (9) class visitations, and (10) consultants.

The major weaknesses of the program were lack of time of the board to participate and too great a distance to travel for many of the frequent meetings.

The strengths of the program are in the fact that changes have occurred in various programs of the college which have enhanced immeasurably the college position. The new-member orientation and systematic mailings have increased the board's effectiveness. The president reported that because of the program the nominating committee changed entirely so that more qualified members are now being elected. Trustees are reimbursed for some expenses involved in the program; however, there is not a budget for in-service education.

INSTITUTION C

Basic Institutional Data

Institution C is a private, fully accredited, church-affiliated college located in a midwestern community. The enrollment is fewer than 2,500 students, who are drawn mainly from surrounding states and the local state. A large percentage of the students enrolled are members of the denomination the college represents. The bachelor's degree is offered in nine fields of specialization.

Board of Trustees Organization

The board of trustees of Institution C consists of 29 members. Thirteen of these members are executives; 7 are educators; 3 are lawyers; 5 are clergymen, and 1 is a financier. Interspersed among these occupations are 16 alumni and 4 women. Nineteen trustees live within a radius of 100 miles of the college, 9 live within 100 to 500 miles, and 1 resides over 1,000 miles away. Two members are over 70 years of age, 7 members are between the ages of 60 and 70, 11 members are between the ages of 40 and 50, and only 1 member falls within the age bracket of 30 to 40 years of age.

Ten trustees have received the bachelor's degree, 3 have attained the master's degree, 4 have earned the doctorate, 4 have been granted honorary degrees, and 8 have not completed a college degree. The board is divided into 4 committees: the building committee, the education committee, the development committee, and the financial committee. The chairmen of each committee compose the executive committee together with the chairman of the board. Additional committees are designed as special needs arise. The president has served as chief executive for 10 years. The trustees are elected for six-year terms and cannot succeed themselves. The board members are elected by a combination of three methods: (1) the church conference delegates; (2) the alumni; and (3) the board itself. The president was interviewed during a one-day visit.

In-Service Education Program

Orientation for New Members. Each new member receives a copy of the minutes of the board for the previous year. The new members are individually welcomed by a personal letter from the president. The new trustees are brought to campus for a one-day seminar in which the president reviews in detail the policies and procedures of the college. A formal installation service follows.

Monthly Mailings. Every month printed literature is mailed to the trustees consisting of (1) the Council for the Advancement of Small Colleges Newsletter; (2) selected higher education journals; and (3) minutes of the executive committee. The journals are selected to increase the board's understanding in aspects of the college program.

Monthly Meetings of Executive Committee. The executive committee meets once a month on campus to maintain a systematic awareness of (1) the programs of the college, (2) the attitudes of faculty and students, and (3) the financial position of the school. In addition, the president chooses various topics to be discussed with the hope that improvement in trusteemanship will result. Members of the administration are invited to attend these meetings to strengthen the awareness of the board in reference to their individual areas of responsibility. This method has proven very satisfactory.

Consultants-Speakers. Consultants are employed to assist the board in understanding a specialized area in which the college lacks resources. Development counsel has been the most widely utilized area for outside help. On occasion speakers from within the college or from neighboring schools are invited to address the board relative to problems that need further exploration.

Trustee Speakers Bureau. The president inaugurated a trustee speakers bureau to represent the college at diversified church groups, alumni meetings, and civic organizations. The bureau is centralized and controlled at the college and keeps the trustees actively engaged in speaking assignments. The president stated that the regularity of speaking assignments has been fairly frequent. The engagements have distinctly broadened the trustee understanding of the college and focused their attention more adeptly on the problems facing higher education.

Individual Conferences. Certain trustees are invited to attend individual conferences with the president. The nature of the conferences is determined by the knowledge perceived by the president to be most lacking on the part of the understanding of individual board members.

Quarterly Meetings. Quarterly the full board meets to conduct legal and financial matters that must be consummated by the total corporate body. The president seeks to make these meetings more than a performance of routine details. The in-service education program helps dictate an agenda that can capture the maximun potential from the time expended. New concepts and ideas concerning curriculum, student affairs, and plant development are placed on the agenda to stimulate and motivate the board to greater effectiveness. Part of the agenda is determined at the monthly executive committee meetings, when topics are selected to provoke discussion and increase the academic growth of each member.

Strengths and Weaknesses of the Program

The major weaknesses of the program are: (1) lack of time, (2) conflict of interest, (3) too much dependence on printed materials, and (4) lack of understanding of fund-raising techniques. The president struggles to overcome the image of being only a fund raiser. The factors that have contributed to the success of the program with the board have been (1) opening of new channels of communication; (2) increased board awareness of the problems and the nature of higher education; (3) more complete understanding of trustee role; (4) stronger support and appreciation of the college staff by the corporate body; (5) creation of new areas of specialization; and (6) all legislation that needed to be approved by the board was passed.

Future Goals of the In-Service Education Program

The president declared that he sought to develop a board that was totally active in the affairs which they must administer. His goal was to create a strongly motivated board designed for service and affluence. He indicated that an establishment of a separate budget for in-service education was one of the immediate goals. He also felt that steps must be taken to permit a proper balance of the methods utilized in the program and the development of greater flexibility on the part of each board member.

Summary of Institution C

The in-service education program is designed to function largely in a centralized manner. The nature of the geographical representation poses difficulty in maintaining consistent centralization.

The president determines and supervises the total in-service education program. The program consists of 7 phases: (1) orientation for new members, (2) monthly mailings, (3) monthly meetings of executive committee, (4) quarterly meetings of the board, (5) consultants-speakers, (6) trustee speakers bureau, and (7) individual conferences.

The weaknesses of the board are attributed to the following factors: (1) lack of time, (2) conflict of interest, (3) too much dependence on printed materials, and (4) lack of understanding of fund-raising techniques.

The success of the program can be measured by these results: (1) opening of new channels of communication; (2) increased board awareness of the problems and the nature of higher education; (3) more complete understanding of trustee role; (4) stronger support and appreciation of the college staff by the board; (5) creation of new areas of specialization; and (6) all legislation that needed to be approved by the board was passed.

The president indicated four future goals of the program. They are: (1) development of a more strongly motivated and affluent board; (2) creation of a separate budget for in-service education of board members; (3) maintain a better balance in the methods utilized in the in-service program; and (4) sustain greater flexibility in each member.

INSTITUTION D

Basic Institutional Data

Institution D is a fully accredited, private college located in a rural community 14 miles from a large metropolitan midwestern city. The college is one of the state's oldest privately supported, church related institutions. Fifty percent of the school's student body come from the local area. Numerous states and several foreign countries are represented among the others. The college offers a liberal-arts program with courses especially adapted to the students preparing for the ministry. No graduate courses are included in the college curriculum. Many of the local students commute from their resident homes.

Board of Trustees Organization

The board of trustees consists of 24 members. Eight members are elected by the general synod of the church and the remaining 16 by self-perpetuation of the board. Nine executives, 4 financiers, 3 clergymen, 2 lawyers, 1 medical physician, 1 dentist, and 2 housewives are represented in the occupations on the board. Two vacancies existed, which had not been filled at the time of the interview. Four alumni are included in the diversification of representation. Fourteen trustees live within a radius of 100 miles of the college, 4 live from 100 to 500 miles distant, and 4 live over 500 miles away. The president did not know the degree attained or ages of the 24 individual members.

The board is organized into four committees: (1) the building committee, (2) development committee, (3) education committee, and (4) financial committee. The chairmen of these committees and the chairman of the board constitute the executive committee. The president has served two years as chief executive and has influenced the selection of three new members who represent the executive field. The president was formerly director of development in the institution he now serves. The chief executive was interviewed during a one-day visit.

In-Service Education Program

Orientation Program for New Members. Newly elected board members are brought to campus for a one-day seminar and conference with the president of the college. The in-service education program for the new members is designed to give the trustees an overview of the college. The president speaks on topics such as admissions standards, student-behavior expectations, curriculum offerings, and graduate requirements. In addition, he discusses the faculty-student-trustee interrelationships. The education committee of the board selects pertinent literature and the board minutes to be sent to each new member to assist the trustee in understanding the academic nature of the college.

Three-Day Retreat. One of the major activities of the in-service education program is a three-day retreat conducted during the summer on the local campus for the full board. An intensive analysis of the various programs is undertaken with the help of the college staff as resource people. Topics such as the role of the liberal arts college, the mission of Institution D, curriculum plans, profile of the students, hopes and plans for Institution D, and the board of trustees in action are discussed at length. Each administrative officer that is responsible for the area addressed is present to act as a resource person during the discussion of the topic. The two retreats that have been held during the president's term in office have proven to be extremely successful; however, no written objective evaluations were available concerning these sessions.

Research. The director of research of the college plays an active role in providing the necessary information to the board relative to research being conducted at Institution D. He functions mainly as a resource person in the in-service education program; however, on occasion he is invited to address the board. The president stated that he is one of the key forces in the improvement program.

Full Board Meetings. At least semiannually the full board meets on the college campus. The interview was conducted during one of the full board meetings. The president is striving to incorporate these meetings into an important phase of the in-service education program. Previous agendas have been saturated with legal and business affairs and not geared at all to the in-service education program. The present agenda, however, contained aspects that were included basically to upgrade the board's vision and understanding of higher education. The response was favorable by the board to the change and the president plans to continue with the newly added approach.

Monthly Meetings of the Executive Committee. Once a month the executive committee meets at a place designated by the chairman of the board. The president is responsible for the agenda; therefore, he uses these meetings as a tool for systematic in-service education. Faculty are invited to many of these meetings to be utilized as part of the improvement program. The affairs are usually conducted in one-half of a day period. The president reports significant growth in the board members in reference to their role and understanding of the varied aspects of higher education.

Monthly Mailings of Printed Materials. Since the board meets only twice a year, printed materials are mailed monthly to them. Much of the present in-service education program must be operated through this vehicle of communication. Selected literature concerning the role of the trustee is included in these mailings. Books, pamphlets, complete journals, and specified articles make up the composition of the printed literature.

Consultants. Counsel is obtained apart from the college to assist the president in designing improvement programs that can advance the trustees' knowledge in an area that evidences apparent weaknesses. Both educational and financial counsel has been secured. The innovations fashioned and motivated by the consultants have enriched the in-service education program.

Faculty-Administration. As has been stated earlier, the faculty and administration play vital roles in being resource personnel for the in-service education program. This role provides excellent direct communication with the board and has elevated their relationships with them. The president remarked that he placed great dependence upon his staff in helping the board understand areas of difficulty.

Budget for the Program. Although there is no item in the budget intended for in-service education for the board, trustees are reimbursed for the expenses incurred in all of their regular meetings.

Evaluation of the Total Program. The evaluation of the in-service education program is done by verbal analysis of the participants to the president. The evaluation is determined either by individual conferences or collective meetings of the board members.

Strengths and Weaknesses of the Program

Lack of time was deemed by the president to be the major weakness in the improvement program. The president also stated that if the selection procedures and qualifications for board membership could be raised, then the program would be enhanced.

The factors that contributed the most to the success of the program were: (1) the realization of the need of the program and the willingness of the board to participate to some extent in it; (2) more individual involvement has been witnessed on the part of the total membership since the program's inception; and (3) equal to this involvement has been the attraction of new members because of the positive reaction to an active program for board participation.

Future Goals of the In-Service Education Program

The future plans of the program include a development of ways to allow more interaction between the board, the faculty, and the students. The second goal of the president is the creation of methods to give more information that presents a total picture of the college and its activities to individual board members.

Summary of Institution D

The in-service education program is both centralized and decentralized. The distance and lack of time for participation of the members do not permit as adequate centralization as is desired.

The in-service education program consists of eight phases : (1) orientation program for new members; (2) a three-day retreat; (3) research; (4) two full board meetings; (5) monthly meetings of the executive committee; (6) monthly mailings of printed materials; (7) consultants; and (8) faculty-administrative speakers.

Trustees are reimbursed for expenses expended for officially called meetings.

Lack of time, inadequate selection procedures, and qualification requirements for membership were felt to be the major weaknesses of the improvement program.

The realization for the need of the program, greater trustee involvement, and attraction of more qualified members were ascertained to be the factors contributing to the success of the in-service education program.

The program is evaluated on a subjective basis by verbal exploration. No objective instruments are employed in the evaluation.

The future goals of the in-service education program are to develop ways to allow greater interaction between the faculty and the students with the trustee and also create new methods of giving more complete information of the college to the board member.

The supervision and determination of the program is finalized by the president, the vice-president, and the academic dean.

INSTITUTION E

Basic Institutional Data

Institution E is a fully accredited, private college located in a large midwestern city of 250,000 people. The school is one of the state's newest liberal arts colleges and is affiliated with a denomination that consists of 7,000 members. The student population of Institution E is approximately 1,800. Fifty percent of the students enroll from the local community and the remaining are drawn from 14 states and three foreign countries. The student body includes a large percentage of commuters who attend both day and evening classes. Although the institution is church related, 44 denominations and faiths are represented. The college offers a liberal arts curriculum with a nursing program affiliated in one of the local hospitals.

Board of Trustees Organization

The membership of the board consists of 23 members. At the time of the interview one vacancy was present in the board membership. Seven executives, 5 clergymen, 2 medical physicians, 5 educators, and 3 financiers compose the occupational categorization. Twelve new members are elected each year to serve one year on the board. Three members maintain an ex-officio status. Fourteen members live within a radius of 100 miles of the college, and 8 members live within 100 to 500 miles. Eight board members are between the ages of 30 and 40, 9 members are between the ages of 50 and 60, and 5 members are over 60 years of age. Four members have earned the bachelor's degree, 1 the master's degree, 4 the doctorate, 2 have honorary degrees, and the status of the others could not be determined. The board is organized into three committees: (1) the building committee; (2) the development committee; and (3) the financial committee. An executive committee is formed from the chairmen of these committees plus the chairman of the board. The president has served as chief administrator for a term of four years. The president and the business manager were interviewed on a one-day visit.

In-Service Education Program

Subcommittees. The in-service education program is designed so that the members of the board are divided into 5 subcommittees: (1) committee on curriculum, (2) admissions committee, (3) student affairs committee, (4) maintenance committee, and (5) public relations committee. One member of the administration and three faculty members are assigned to each committee. The committees are so structured that a depth analysis of each area can be undertaken. The administrators chosen for the committee are selected by the president. The dean of the faculty appoints faculty members to each committee. The meetings are held on a two-day basis, normally starting with Friday evening. The agendas for the committee meetings are planned by the faculty and administrative representatives. The methodology employed on each committee varies, but usually the administrator initiates the opening discussions. During the process of accreditation, the president addressed the committees collectively then dismissed them into the subcommittees to discuss individual ramifications of his address.

Two pivotal men in the in-service education program relative to the subcommittees are the chairman and vice chairman of the board. They are permanent members of the board and are major professors in two large universities of the local state. The president states that their brilliant knowledge has pioneered ideas that have brought significant advances in the trustees' perception. Their sophisticated educational "know how" has widened the program's concepts immensely. The president accredits the rapid progress of the board to the educational stature and performance of these two men.

The committees were rotated on a regular basis so that every member could be exposed to the various facets of college activity.

The president attested that the structuring of the committees and using that structure as the main method of in-service education was the most efficient and profitable way.

Appropriate printed materials or resource people were invited as needed.

Committee on Curriculum. The college had been granted accreditation four months prior to the on campus interview. The in-service education program for the curriculum committee demanded that tremendous strides be undertaken in the committee efforts so that the quality of the curriculum could be worthy of accreditation. Although normally the college administration initiated the discussion in the committees, the chairman and vice-chairman of the board guided the discussions in curriculum. The granting of accreditation was a paramount result of their collective efforts. Printed materials, discussion of the president's lecture, and case study analysis were part of the procedures followed.

Committee on Admissions. Institution E evidenced a rapid expansion in enrollment since its foundation. The admissions problems connected with swift expansion provided the main areas for discussion in this committee designed for board improvement. The communication in this committee resulted in a broader understanding by the board on the vast ramifications of admissions standards in a church college serving a local community. The president reported that the requests processed by the admissions officer became more easily understood and were adopted unanimously at the full board annual meeting.

Committee on Student Affairs. The dean of students usually chaired the meeting and fashioned thought-provoking discussions on the topic, "Expectations of Student Behavior Among Resident and Non-Resident Students." The college faced an interesting challenge of achieving a proper balance in the standards required of all students. The church affiliation and religious perspective which had originally established unique student behavioral requirements are now being shattered by the cosmopolitan backgrounds and experiences of the diversified student body. The in-service education program seeks to probe this problem more deeply and find satisfactory solutions to it.

Committee on Public Relations. The president chairs this committee and because of the lack of development personnel, he also includes development under public relations. The improvement program patterns the agenda to assist the board in communicating to the church groups a more thorough understanding of the delicate balance between church ownership and community responsibility. The institution is located in a community that seeks to structure the college to one that mainly serves the community. Large gifts from the industrial corporations in the community have sometimes altered the original objectives of the college. The president stated that the lively discussion of this topic has helped in arriving at wise and valid decisions.

Committee on Maintenance. Time did not permit an extensive analysis of the interworkings of this committee. Plant facilities and the operation of them were the major areas of discussion.

Full Board Meetings. Three times a year the full board meets. The motivation that was evident in the subcommittees is carried through to the full board meetings. The in-service education program that was initiated in the subcommittees is also designed to facilitate the board to utilize part of the full board meetings for in-service education. The president affirmed that "Every board meeting now has an educational function."

Advisory Committee. Assisting in the in-service education program is an advisory committee composed of people representing diverse occupational backgrounds. The entire group meets once a year but individuals or groups of individuals are used as resource people to strengthen the improvement program. The wealth of experience of these individuals has added measurably to the program.

Subjective evaluations are made of the improvement program and the president reports that an average program exists. No budget is as yet allocated for in-service education.

Strengths and Weaknesses of the Program

The development of greater intercommunication among the subgroups has been evaluated as the major factor in the success of the program. Irregular attendance has hindered the success of the improvement activities.

Future Goals of the In-Service Education Program

The future goals of the program are to attract more qualified members to be elected to the board so that broader ramifications of the program can be attained.

Summary of Institution E

The in-service education program of Institution E is mainly centralized with its functioning focused on campus activities. The administration, with the leadership of the chairman and vice-chairman of the board, determine and supervise the program.

The improvement program encompasses three phases: (1) subcommittees; (2) full board meetings; and (3) advisory committee as resource people.

The subcommittees are organized into the committee on curriculum, the admissions committee, the student-affairs committee, the maintenance committee, and the public relations committee.

The president appoints one administrator and the dean appoints three faculty members to each committee.

No budget or objective evaluative instruments are engaged in the improvement program.

The major strength of the program has been the development of greater intercommunication among the groups.

Irregular attendance has been the major factor hindering the success of the program.

The future goal of the program is to attract more qualified members to serve on the board who in turn will enhance the total aspect and activities of the improvement efforts.

INSTITUTION F

Basic Institutional Data

Institution F is a fully accredited, private, independently controlled college located in an industrial center in one of the eastern seaboard states. The student enrollment is less than 5,000 drawn from many states in the union but mainly residing in one of the eastern coastal states. The college is a liberal-arts school, yet the institution is known mainly for the extensive research constantly being undertaken for several national pharmaceutical manufacturers.

Board of Trustee Organization

The board of trustees of Institution F has 25 members. Seven financiers, 13 executives, 1 lawyer, 1 medical physician, and 3 educators represent the occupational backgrounds of the members. Six women and 3 alumni are among the membership. Twenty-two trustees live within 100 miles of the college and three live from 100 to 500 miles away. Four members are between the ages of 30 and 40, 5 members are between the ages of 40 and 50, 7 trustees are within the age bracket of 50–60, and 10 members are over 60 years of age. Ten of the board members have received their bachelor's degree, 1 the master's degree, 3 the earned doctorate, 6 have been granted honorary degrees, and 5 had not achieved any college degrees. The board is organized into three committees: (1) the building committee, (2) the development committee, and (3) the financial-aid committee. The chairmen of these committees plus the chairman of the board constitute the board executive committee. The president has served Institution F as chief administrator 16 years. Twenty new members have been added since he became president. Six financiers, 9 executives, 1 lawyer, 1 medical physician, and 3 educators represent the backgrounds of the new members who were selected. Three alumni are included in the representation. The board is self-perpetuating and the president affirmed that he had exerted strong influence in the selection of the new members.

In-Service Education Program

Orientation Program for New Members. Each new member of the board is presented a copy of Myron Wicke's *Handbook for a Trustee,* and is given opportunity to discuss the book at an individual conference with the president. Many of the conferences take the form of a weekend as the guest in the home of the president. The objectives of the college and the bylaws of the institution are thoroughly reviewed with the new member. On occasion faculty and administration are invited to participate in the individual orientation. A brief overview of the in-service education program of the year is presented and opportunity for interaction is always given. The rapport established between the board and the president has been excellent. The president attributes this largely to the informal orientation which initiates the board to the college and the in-service education program.

Special Committee on Long-Range Planning. A special committee is appointed as a subcommittee of the board. This committee is assigned the task of being the group who assists the president and the chairman of the board in designing programs for the improvement of the college. The president also utilizes the group to provide ideas and activities for in-service education. The committee specified three areas to be the major focus of discussion throughout the year and these areas were chosen with a basic goal for upgrading the knowledge of each individual board member relative to them. The areas chosen are (1) fund raising, (2) fiscal problems, (3) curriculum development.

The president reports that when he took office the board admitted that they had been a failure and wanted a program that could improve their effectiveness. The work of the subcommittee has proven to be the most respected and capable instrument in enhancing their effectiveness.

Weekly Conferences with the Chairman of the Board. The president ascertained that the leadership of the in-service education program must be initially motivated by the president and the chairman of the board. He felt that the motivation maintained and exercised by these two officeis would be the primary factor in the success or failure of the improvement program. To assure an increasing motivation, the president established a weekly meeting with the chairman of the board. Although the location and the type of meeting constantly changes, the regularity of the meeting only ceases during a vacation of one of the members. The activities of the program, the response to these activities, and changes in procedures and methodology employed in the program are discussed during the conferences. When areas need further clarification or exploration, selected faculty or administrators attend the meeting. The president believes these meetings have accomplished 7 results: (1) strengthened the support of the chairman of the board to the college programs; (2) established basic principles and guidelines for more trustee involvement in the in-service education program; (3) increased and maintained a better motivation for the improvement program; (4) broadened the knowledge of the chairman of the board in reference to higher education and the college he serves (the board chairman changes after serving two terms); (5) systematic communication has kept channels open to the college which has prohibited any major crises on the board; (6) strengthened immensely the leadership ability of the president; and (7) one of the major factors in achieving high morale in the paramount leadership of the board.

Small-Group Discussions. The president stated that one of the ways of increasing the board adeptness is to conduct small-group meetings with them regularly throughout the year. Since most of the trustees live within 100 miles of the college it has been desired that all members could attend most conferences. The regularity of attendance has not been as good as had been anticipated; however, the meetings progressed quite satisfactorily. A college social, cultural, or athletic event is the primary motivation facilitated to attract the members to campus. These conferences are conducted on an informal basis with the president and chairman having planned the topics of discussion in their weekly meetings. The president always attends, but the chairman of the board is not required to attend every conference. Periodically one of the committee is invited to campus for this interchange; however, the main emphasis is to obtain a wider representation. Resource materials or personnel are included when the president or chairman deem it necessary. Some of the meetings are parties in the president's home.

Attendance at Professional Meetings. Normally every year trustees are invited to attend professional meetings with the president. Although time, availability, and expense warrant only a small representation, the president seeks to involve as many of the members as circumstances permit. These meetings are part of the in-service education program, and participation in them has significantly given an outside dimension to the program.

Printed Materials. Books, pamphlets, professional journals, and individual articles are dispensed to the membership of the board on a fairly regular basis. The type of material is selected by a variety of people but always channeled through the president's office. No communication takes place with the board without the president's approval or knowledge beforehand. Much of the printed material functions as a resource in the board individual or small group conferences.

Research Consultants for the Board. In areas of specialization which verify a larger degree of proficiency than is represented on the college staff, research personnel are obtained from the outside to investigate these assigned areas of study. Financial problems with an emphasis on fund-raising techniques have required the most consistent necessity for counsel. During periods of self-study educational consultants are obtained to inform and acclimate the board to the processes involved.

Individual Conferences. The president advocates a continuous stream of communication with the board as the underlying method of in-service education. Quite frequently this takes the form of individual conferences with members of the board. Dinners, office calls, weekend visits, campus lectures, social or athletic events, business trips, and vacation guests are part of the activities utilized in the individual conferences. The main purposes of these conferences are to (1) strengthen areas of weaknesses identified in the board member in a basic area of specialization; (2) achieve a better understanding of the board member; (3) encourage greater individual participation and involvement by the board member; and (4) assist the board member to understand more completely his role.

Executive Committee Meetings. The meetings of the executive committee are employed as an important phase of the total improvement program. The executive committee meets on a regular basis with the president. The president and the chairman of the board create methods that can serve as tools for board improvement. Resource personnel, slides, lectures, case studies, professional articles, and books are implemented into the in-service education aspects with the executive committee. Subjective evaluations are made of each meeting.

Full Board Meetings. Quarterly the full board meets to complete corporate affairs of the college. These meetings deal mainly with business matters; therefore, the president invites the business manager to take part. One of the glaring weaknesses of the board when the president assumed his role was relative to their business understanding. An improvement program geared to the talents of the business manager was conceived and has distinctly enlarged the board's business understanding since its inception. The president declared that the most articulate and sophisticated individual in the entire in-service education program is the business manager. The business manager came from a lengthy experience as a teacher and devises unique methods to present information to the board which gains lasting results. The president stated that his greatest personal satisfaction with the in-service education program originates with the performance of the business manager. The business manager's ability has advanced the business phase of the program far beyond the president's hopes.

Strengths and Weaknesses of the Program

The major factors in the success of the program have been: (1) excellent types of continuous communication maintained in the program; (2) the qualified resource personnel participating in the specialized phases of the program; (3) the desire of the board to facilitate programs for their own improvement; and (4) high morale of participation.

The major factors that have hindered the program are (1) lack of time, (2) lack of a budget for in-service education, and (3) lack of objective instruments to evaluate the program.

Future Goals of the In-Service Education Program

The goals of the program to be consummated in the future are as follows: (1) obtain broader geographical distribution among the membership; (2) educate them more effectively in areas of weaknesses; and (3) devise more unique methods to present information and materials.

Summary of Institution F

Institution F maintains an in-service education program centralized in the authority of the president and chairman of the board. These two men provide the impetus and motivation for a systematic, imaginative in-service program. Weekly conferences between these two men are held to increase the effectiveness of the improvement program. These meetings have accomplished seven results: (1) strengthened the support of the chairman of the board to the total college program; (2) established basic principles and guidelines for more trustee involvement in the in-service education program; (3) increased and maintained a better motivation for in-service education; (4) broadened the knowledge of the chairman of the board relative to higher education and the college he serves; (5) provided a means of avoiding major crisis on the board; (6) strengthened immensely the leadership ability of the president; and (7) contributed highly to the morale evidenced in the leaders of the board.

The remaining aspects of the program are organized into nine phases. The activities and resources employed are basically (1) orientation program for new members; (2) a special committee on long-range planning; (3) small-group discussions; (4) attendance at professional meetings; (5) printed materials; (6) research consultants; (7) individual conferences; (8) executive committee meetings; and (9) full board meetings quarterly.

The major factors contributing to the success of the program have been: (1) excellent types of continuous communication maintained in the program; (2) the qualified resource personnel participating in the specialized phases of the program; (3) the desire of the board to facilitate programs for their own improvement; and (4) the high morale evidenced on the part of the participants.

The major factors hindering the program are simply (1) lack of time; (2) lack of a budget for in-service education; and (3) lack of objective instruments to evaluate the program.

The president stated three future goals of the in-service education program. They are listed in order of importance as (1) obtain broader geographical distribution among the membership; (2) educated board more effectively in areas of weakness; and (3) devise more unique methods to present the in-service education materials and information.

INSTITUTION G

Basic Institutional Data

Institution G is a private, church related college located in one of the largest midwestern cities. The college has not been accredited but significant steps are under way to hasten the granting of accreditation. Institution G has three separate schools: an academy, an undergraduate school, and a seminary. The equivalent of a president administers each academic school. The undergraduate school on which the study is based has an enrollment of fewer than 1,500 students. Thirty percent of the students are drawn from the local area and the remaining represent 20 states and five foreign countries. Eighty percent of the students are members of the church denomination the college serves. The remaining 20 percent are diversified into 12 religious denominations and faiths. Four years ago a complete liberal arts program was added to the curriculum.

Board of Trustees Organization

Institution G is governed by the board of education of the church affiliation. The board is composed of 21 members, each of whom serves for three years. Seven members are elected at each annual church conference to which the board of education is directly responsible. Ex-officio members include the president of the church denomination, the presidents of the seminary and college, the church conference chairman and vice chairman. Among the members are represented by occupation 8 executives, 10 clergymen, 1 lawyer, 1 medical physician, and 1 politician. Eight alumni are included in the representation. Ten trustees live within a radius of 100 miles of the college, 9 live from 100 to 500 miles away, 4 live from 500 to 1,000 miles away, and 2 live over 1,000 miles distant. Eight members are between the ages of 60 to 70, 9 are between the ages of 40 and 50, and 4 are between the ages of 30 and 40. Four members have received the bachelor's degree, 3 have attained the master's degree, 2 have earned the doctorate, one has been granted an honorary degree, and the remainder have not achieved any college degrees.

The board is organized into 4 committees: (1) the building committee; (2) the development committee; (3) the education committee; and (4) the financial committee. An executive committee is composed of each committee chairman and the chairman of the board. The president has served as chief administrator of the college for seven years. Eleven new members have been elected during his term of office. He was able to influence to some extent the selection of the new members. The new members' occupational backgrounds represent: 4 executives; 4 clergymen; 1 lawyer; 1 medical physician; and 1 politician. Four alumni the among the new members. The interviews were conducted with the president and the dean of faculty during a one-day campus visit.

In-Service Education Program

Consultant. Upon the inception of the in-service education program a consultant was retained to assist the president and dean of the faculty in determining and supervising the program. The major emphasis of the improvement program has centered in the vision and activities designed by the consultant. The in-service education activities focus upon four main areas: (1) organizational tasks; (2) development tasks; (3) educational tasks; and (4) spiritual tasks. Methods of orientation to the four main areas are: (1) problem orientation; (2) preventive orientation; and (3) corrective orientation. The program is designed to function on a regular three-year basis with the consultant giving two days a month for on-campus board exploration. The main goals of the program are: (1) achieve greater participation and involvement of board members in service to the college; (2) increase their understanding of their role; (3) gain broader knowledge of higher education; and (4) assist the college to achieve accreditation.

Organizational Tasks. The approach to the in-service education program relative to organizational responsibility has utilized printed materials and group discussion procedures. The consultant perceived that the board lacked understanding of their organizational role and is attempting to eliminate these misunderstandings by personal confrontation and selected reading analysis. The results have been very satisfactory and similar plans will be implemented in the future.

Development Tasks. Prior to the inception of the in-service program the board determined that trustees would require that all development activities be conducted by the president. The in-service education program has reversed that concept and now the board is beginning to assume the major portion of the responsibility for fund raising. Case study analysis and firsthand experiences are the two basic methods adapted to increase the board's effectiveness in this area.

Educational Tasks. A self-study of the entire academic program has been undertaken so that a satisfactory quality can be achieved that meets the accreditation requirements. Most of the in-service education program centers upon this area. The board has been divided among faculty committees which are analyzing in depth aspects of the academic curriculum. Lectures, panels, slides, outside speakers, and printed materials are all employed in this in-depth investigation. Representatives of the board meet monthly with faculty and administrative members to cooperatively pursue assigned topics of responsibility. The discussions that have been effected and the changes that have been made in the curriculum attest to the positive aspects of the improvement program. Some personality conflicts have developed between the board and faculty members but they have been of short duration.

Spiritual Tasks. Institution G, being a church-related college, is developing means for more effective procurement of a spiritually saturated environment. One of the easier aspects of the in-service education program is designing tasks for increased spiritual and religious understanding. The backgrounds of the trustees permit excellent interaction in this area. The homogeneous religious makeup of the faculty, staff, and trustees provides sufficient motivation for studying extensively the vast ramifications of a tightly controlled, church-related institution.

Executive Committee Meetings. The in-service education program utilized the executive committee meetings as a facet of the improvement program. The executive committee meets regularly and has become very active in the in-service education activities. Most of the administrative officers participate in the discussions when their area of responsibility is represented on the agenda. Written reports, lectures, and discussions are the main types of resource functioning in the in-service program for the executive committee.

Full Board Meetings. Four times a year the full board meets as a corporate body. The consultant has not designed as yet an extensive program for the board when it convenes. The president states that 21 regular members are too many to plan an in-service education for the entire group. Future procedures are being evaluated that might prove effective with a large group.

Meetings with the Chairman of the Board. Regular meetings are conducted with the chairman of the board to fully inform and involve him with the in-service education activities. To maintain regularity, telephone conversations are sometimes employed.

On-Campus Visitations. In addition to the faculty-trustee committee meetings there are personal staff conferences selected by the president. The purpose of the individual conferences is to provide a board member with direct analysis of an area of specialization. The follow-up to the meetings is held many times without the president's knowledge and has created a personality conflict.

Budget for In-Service Education. The largest budget for in-service education is found in Institution G, which as stated earlier, is the only nonaccredited college having an in-service education program. For the total improvement program $5,000 is expended. Most of this amount, however, is budgeted for the consultant's fees and services. In the future it is anticipated that this budget will be increased substantially.

Future Plans of the In-Service Education Program

The future plans of the in-service education program are threefold: (1) more involvement of the board in the planning of the program; (2) less emphasis on trivial details; and (3) increase in the in-service education budget.

Strengths and Weaknesses of the Program

Although the program is relatively new the major weakness of it is trying to achieve broader and more effective methods in developing the board members' understanding in areas of most difficulty. Adequate methods have not clearly been finalized.

The factor that has contributed most to the success of the in-service education program has been the ability of the consultant and his wealth of experience that he brings to the program.

Summary of Institution G

The determination and supervision of the in-service education program rests mainly with the president, the dean, and a consultant. The consultant actually plans the major phases of the program and directs the resource personnel to be employed in it. The program is divided into four tasks of exploration: (1) organizational tasks; (2) development tasks; (3) educational tasks; and (4) spiritual tasks. The approaches to these areas involve three methods of orientation: (1) problem orientation, (2) preventive orientation, and (3) corrective orientation.

Other aspects of the program include effective committee meetings, quarterly board meetings, regular conferences with the chairman of the board, and on-campus visitations.

A budget of $5,000 is maintained for in-service education and is expended for the most part to cover the consultant's fees and expenses.

The factors that have contributed to the success of the relatively new in-service education program have been the ability of the consultant and the wealth of experience that he brings to the college. The major factors hindering the success of the program have been the lack of finalization for efficient and effective methods for correction of board weaknesses.

CHAPTER 7

Educating and Evaluating Trustees

The dismissal of Clark Kerr as president of the University of California by the board of regents has once again vividly demonstrated the power and control governing boards have over institutions of higher learning.

These powers which are legally constituted can be a major vehicle for the growth or the demise of a college or university. It is imperative, therefore, that governing boards exhibit the highest degree of educational readiness when they exercise their role as decision makers. The results of a board's decision can have long-range effects on the nature of an institution and could have a profound influence on the direction of higher education.

A question then arises: What assurance does the public have that the most appropriate decisions are determined by those charged with the responsibility to govern the academic community?

In the preceding chapter we saw clearly the method of answering that question—in-service education. Based upon that analysis, the author recommends the following for consideration.

IN-SERVICE EDUCATION[1]

*All presidents in colleges and universities should inaugurate and implement an in-service education program for their boards of trustees.

*The president and the chairman of the board should bear full responsibility for the success or failure of the in-service education program.

The planning and the determination of the in-service programs must by made by representatives from the board and the president's staff. The executive committee of the college and the executive committee of the board can serve as a cooperative committee organizing and effecting a

[1] Orley R. Herron, "Keep Educating Your Trustees," *College and University Business Journal*, Vol. 42, No. 4 (April 1967), pp. 83–84.

program for in-service education. If the organizational structure of the college and board does not include executive committees, then the president of the college and the chairman of the board can select a special committee composed of college staff and board members. Co-chairmen should administer the committee. The chairmanship should be shared by a board member and a college staff person. Each institution's needs are unique; therefore, a program must be designed with these individual needs in view. Ideas and concepts from programs of other schools may be applied to ensure greater success and variety in the in-service education program. Objectives and goals of the in-service education program should be determined and they should complement the objectives of the college. The activities of the in-service program must be maintained with a high degree of continuity and regularity.

The role of the trustee is a part-time one; therefore, participation in the in-service education program must be on a volunteer basis. Qualifications for a college board member, however, should include willingness and agreement to participate extensively in the program. Detailed orientation to the in-service education program must augment every new member's inauguration as a trustee.

In-service education should be geared to equip the board with the necessary information and knowledge to enable it to pursue within its maximum potential the objectives of the college.

Contents of the program should expose the members of the board to some common problems of higher education so that they can increase their individual perception of higher education.

Strong motivation and momentum should be effected and continued by the leadership of the in-service education program if maximum results are to be achieved. Resource personnel from within the college of the board should be utilized in the program.

Acknowledged imaginary barriers of communication must be eliminated so that an open channel of communication can exist. Frequent regularity in communication should be maintained among the in-service education leadership.

At least part, with the goal of underwriting all, of the personal expenses incurred by the trustees in the in-service education program should be included in the total budget of the college. Ideally, a separate budget for in-service education of the board of trustees should be formulated and itemized in the annual budget of the institution.

The in-service education program must be evaluated individually by each board member. Project and immediate needs must underlie the design of the in-service education program.

Activities utilized in the in-service education program should include: (1) On-campus visitations with maximum facilitation of trustee's time determined prior to the visitation. A variety of experiences should dominate regularly planned visitations. (2) Personnel confrontations by the board members with selected representatives of the faculty, the administration, and the students. (3) A preschool workshop engaging members of the college to interact with the board member's effectiveness and understanding of his role as college trustee.

Frequent communication by the president with every member of the board can take the form of committee meetings, group seminars, individual conferences, telephone conversations, or periodic mailings. Once a year the president should meet personally with each member of the board to discuss activities affecting his trustee responsibilities.

A high level of frequency should be maintained in the regularity of communication with the chairman of the board. The president and the chairman are deemed the two most important people in the in-service education program.

Annual intraschool workshops should be held apart from the campus to ensure privacy and uninterrupted scheduling for the participants. Resource personnel should be invited to assist the trustees in analysis of areas that require special investigation.

Every meeting of the board should utilize to some extent in-service education. The agenda of the board determines the major discussions of the meetings; therefore, the persons responsible for the agenda must consider the in-service education program a cohesive element of each meeting.

Broad opportunities should be provided for each board member to interact with the students. Participation in class lectures, chapel services, convocations, social gatherings, student government meetings, and residence-hall seminars are some methods that can increase the interaction.

Encourage trustee attendance at professional meetings. Periodically, though not necessarily yearly, board members should accompany college staff to selected professional meetings. The expense incurred by these meetings should be underwritten by the college. Speaking assignments and fund-raising solicitations should be included in the in-service education activities to encourage greater participation and understanding of the college by the board. Cooperative participation by a college staff member and the trustee can enhance each activity assigned.

The resource materials employed in the in-service education program should include a variety of printed materials and visual aids. Printed materials ought to be mailed on a regular basis with defined objectives for each mailing. Modern techniques of visual aids can be utilized very satisfactorily in group or full board meetings.

Studies relative to in-service education programs for trustees should be undertaken to permit more reliable and valid formulation of adequate in-service education programming. Measuring instruments that can provide a more objective means for such evaluation must be designed.

Comprehensive evaluation should be undertaken of qualifications, election procedures, and occupational representation of board members. Institutional changes in policy and representation are vitally needed.

In-service education is only a beginning in the professional development of boards but it is a significant beginning and one in which we encourage every governing board that desires excellence.

GUIDELINES—IN-SERVICE EDUCATION

From the analysis of in-service education of trustees it can be summarized as follows:

1. In-service education is infrequently utilized as a method for improvement of the ability of the boards of trustees in colleges and universities. The programs in operation are relatively new and basically unfinalized.

2. There are general procedures and basic principles involved in the inauguration of an in-service education program.

3. The determination, supervision, and motivation of the in-service education program is primarily the responsibility of the president and the chairman of the board.

4. The facilitation of an in-service education program is usually shared by many individuals apart from the designated president and chairman of the board.

5. An in-service education program, to operate successfully, must be designed to function within the objectives of the college.

6. Occupational responsibilities limit the extent of the availability and the on-campus participation of individual board members. Many board members involved in lay professions must give the greater portion of their time to their vocations to maintain successful enterprises. The level of personal financial accomplishment is a major factor in being selected as a member of a college board of trustees, and continued maintenance of that level presents many conflicts to annual scheduling of in-service education activities.

7. Flexibility is essential in structuring a program for in-service education activities; however, rigid formulation does not necessarily preclude success in in-service education activities. The extracurricular aspect of board status normally warrants restraint in rigid demands for board involvement.

8. With the exception of college staff, no board member receives membership on a full-time basis. Therefore, in-service education activities ought to be conducted on a volunteer basis.

9. The sharing of the planning of the in-service education activities with members of the board, and in particular the chairman, assures a higher degree of cooperation and support in the in-service education program.

10. The role of the board and college staff as one of employer and employee can close channels of communication if class distinctiveness is emphasized greatly in the in-service education program.

11. In-service orientation activities inaugurate very clearly the projected aspects of the in-service education program.

12. The historic lay representation on the boards since the Civil War affirms the need for an adequate in-service education program.

13. There have been relatively few major attempts to evaluate the interworkings and effectiveness of in-service education programs by objective instruments or intensive research studies.

14. Presidents rely heavily on the individual board members to increase board adeptness by personally motivated means and methods. These methods are normally pursued without college guidance or supervision.

15. A variety of in-service education activities are applicable to most institutions. The uniqueness of the organization of Catholic college boards can dictate a difference in the type of activities from non-Catholic boards.

16. Board members need a more thorough understanding of their role relative to their responsibilities and the expectations in the execution of those responsibilities.

17. Common problems face most presidents in designing programs to improve the performance and educational understanding of their boards of trustees.

18. A similar pattern of occupation diversification is represented on most boards of trustees.

19. Only a small portion of the trustee's time has been geared to activities created for professional growth.

20. Lack of adequate analysis of the educational aspects of the college at the board of trustee level affects the nature of trusteemanship. The colleges that neglect proper attention to the academic pursuits tend to consider the institution more as a manufacturing enterprise rather than an organization founded to train young men and women in higher education.

21. The qualifications for membership and the methods of selection to the board limit decisively the quality of the in-service education program.

22. The size of the board can affect the regularity of full board in-service education activities.

23. College boards of trustees have not availed themselves fully of the opportunities, resource personnel, activities, or printed materials that can be utilized for improvement maturation.

24. Lack of time and availability of trustees hinder the formulation of a continuous in-service education program.

25. Presidents of colleges gain more support and better rapport from the board by conducting in-service education programs.

26. In-service education programs can be implemented and continued without large expenditures of money.

27. Trustees are willing to spend monies to cover minimum personal expenses involved in the in-service education program. The enlargement of the activities and the increase in participation by the board demand that personal expenses be underwritten by the college so that future involvement is not hindered.

28. Very few trustees take the necessary time to analyze thoroughly the printed materials included in the in-service education program. The level of professional readiness determines quite frequently the response of each board member to the printed materials.

EVALUATING TRUSTEES[2]

Evaluation of trustees, both individually and collectively, is vital to the building of a strong board of trustees. For the purposes of a short-course evaluation of a board, the following 17 general questions could be used:

1. How well do your board members understand the goals of your institution?

A board must understand the goals and objectives of the institution clearly and succinctly. It is the responsibility of the college staff to ensure that understanding. The administration should never assume a board understands the goals of the institution until careful and consistent communication has made ideal understanding possible. Robert M. Merry proposed: "To ensure a trustee's effectiveness lead him to a proper understanding of the institution . . . and see to it that he has fun doing his job."[3]

2. How well equipped is your board to achieve these goals?

Boston's Richard Cardinal Cushing remarked recently: "It makes no sense to appoint people to a university board who know absolutely

---

[2] Orley R. Herron, "10 Ways To Measure Trustee Effectiveness," *College and University Business Journal*, Vol. 42, No. 6 (June 1967), pp. 53–54.

[3] R. E. Merry, "How to Orient and Train Trustees," *Liberal Education*, Vol. XLV (October 1959), pp. 373–381.

nothing about running a university."[4] A board can understand the goals of an institution very well. However, if they do not have the ability to achieve these goals, then there is a definite need to make some changes. Understanding and doing are two different and extremely important vectors. They must coincide—and can if the board members are adequately selected.

3. How well do you think your trustees understand their role as board members?

S. U. Martorana remarked: "It is imperative to the continued resource growth and development of American higher education that boards of trustees, college staff members, and the public at large understand the role of trustees in governing colleges and universities. As stewards acting for larger interests in the society, the trustees themselves must maintain an awareness and understanding of the changing character, not only of the institution or institutions they direct but also of higher education as a totality."[5]

Trustees have a collective role, yet they have individual roles that must be clearly spelled out and then directed for a maximum effort. Some of the misunderstanding of roles occurs because the trustee and the properly designated officials did not take the necessary time orientation. Colleges pride themselves in orientation programs for new students but often fail miserably with orientation of new board members.

4. Have the needs of the college been defined so board members are selected to meet these needs?

Boards of trustees are represented by the doers, the doubters, the donors, and the deciders. The DOERS usually make sure the work gets done and give liberally of their time. The DOUBTERS are the dissenters who regularly bring the negative approach to positive, progressive programs. The DONORS give generously so that the financial and physical needs are brought to fruition. The DECIDERS are the power structure of the board who make the decisions.

A board of trustees may have members representing each or all of these types. The important point is to define the needs of the college in a long-range manner and select trustees equal to those needs. There is nothing worse than a board selected poorly to meet the challenge of a potentially exciting program. In contrast, there is nothing more gratifying than a board selected that is equal to the demands of the future. That type of board and institution is one to watch because it is going places.

4 "Time for Boy Scouts?" *Time*, Vol. 62 (April 28, 1967).
5 S.V., *College Boards of Trustees* (Washington, D.C., 1963), p. 1.

5. Do you have an in-service education program for your board members?

One of the greatest weaknesses among college trustees is the lack of a systematic educational program to strengthen the understanding of their role and their responsibilities as stewards of an educational institution. The chairman of the board and the president of the institution are obligated to design, direct, supervise a continuous self-improvement program. Board decisions must be reasonable, rational, and based on a deep understanding of higher education. The in-service education program can give the board the basis of educational adeptness upon which to make decisions.

6. What steps have been taken to reduce or eliminate the weaknesses on the board?

The weaknesses of the board should be identified and then proper steps initiated to eliminate these weaknesses. Weaknesses have a way of being self-perpetuating and that does nothing more than to hinder the progress of an institution. If a board is willing to expend the effort, the cost, and the power, weaknesses can be eliminated readily. Don't put off, however, until future years the solution to problems that need immediate attention. The problems will not go away. They will grow to the extent that solutions will be extremely difficult to achieve.

7. Who plans the agenda for board meetings?

The agenda of the board is one of the most significant aspects in the development of a strong, flexible, and solid corporate body. The kinds of information presented to the board will determine to a great extent the type of board one desires them to be. The board should be exposed to information from all disciplines and also participants in some level of the decision-making process regarding these areas. If the board deals only, for example, with the business aspects of an institution, then other important areas will suffer when presented for board consideration. A well-balanced agenda will pay off in the long run.

8. What members of the faculty, administration, and student body meet regularly with the board at its regular meetings?

Board members need to have contact with more than a selected few officers of the administration to understand the complexities of today's academic mind. Don't be afraid to permit the board to meet in informal sessions as well as regular meetings with the students, faculty, and staff. If the task is education, then contact with various diversified groups is essential.

9. Is there a proper balance of professional backgrounds represented on the board?

Colleges differ with respect to goals, needs, and objectives. The board must represent these concepts clearly in the types of backgrounds that are brought to bear in its membership. Too high a percentage of one background dominating a board is not good for a well-balanced membership. Evaluate the board relative to backgrounds and then select the occupations that are needed to give the board the proper balance.

10. Is the board of trustees doing the job that it is incorporated to do?

The board can legally enter all phases of activity on college campus and make decisions relative to those areas. Good boards designed for maximum effectiveness, however, will know when and to whom responsibilities should be delegated, when to exercise their power as a corporate body, when they are "meddling" and when they are managing, and above all, what they want to do and how to go about doing it. The trustees have a mission to perform and it is the task of the college to see that they do it. The trustees do not have the time to get waylaid with affairs that could best be handled by others. It is a necessity that a trustee's role be designed for the greatest utilization of his time, talent, and effort. If the trustees are doing an extraordinary job, it will be more than apparent.

11. Do you want an active, involved board?

The institution must ask quite candidly whether or not it wants an active, involved governing board. Such a board can bring many new dimensions and ramifications to the college. There are various proponents that are speaking strongly against the development of an active board, thinking that such a board will be detrimental today. This need not be the case because an active, involved board can spell progress for an institution. The strategic question is where and how they are to be active and involved. If they are to duplicate services already in operation, then they are not a help. But if they become identified with dimensions that need their judgment, energy, and advice, their work is positive and worthwhile. The president and his staff can assist in channeling the energies of the board into positive activities that are beneficial to the institution. The president, his staff, and the faculty may not honestly want an active board of trustees. If that is their attitude then it is certain they will work energetically against the development of a board becoming one. Whatever administrative posture is assumed, it must become involved, after careful analysis so that it will promote the best interests of the institution. It is quite true that the type of institution—and really the type of trustees that are governing—is the measuring stick on involvement. The boards that can wisely handle active involvement should have it, and those that cannot should not be encouraged to do so without adequate programming.

12. How available are the trustees?

Trustees need to be available for meetings, consultations, and other college activities if they are to serve as stewards of the academic enterprise. Absentee landlordism is not beneficial for any institution. There are notable exceptions to this when a "named" figure brings notoriety and prestige to an institution by just listing his name as a trustee. All "names" and no workers will get you nowhere; however, there is a middle ground and the college must plot that course. Distance, though important, is not too crucial a question because this is the day of supersonic transportation. Most trustees can find transportation to come to the meetings. Their accessibility and availability is the key. Select trustees who can be available for the regularly required meetings. All trustees, no matter what background they may assume, are important to the discussion of the business of the institution. Trustees should not be selected if they do not have the competence, concern, and availability to serve on the board. Too regularly board members abdicate their responsibilities by not attending the meetings, and their talents are then minimal to the institution. The president as the guardian of the trustees time will use his wisest discretion not to convene at an improper time and for unnecessary board meetings. The trustees for the most part have other duties to perform and greatly desire to utilize their institutional responsibilities expertly.

13. How well equipped and prepared for the meetings are the trustees and the appropriate staff?

There is no substitute for preparation. It takes time, talents, and programming. If higher education is to continue to be a significant force in the world, then adequate preparation for its undertakings is a prerequisite. The planning of the agenda was considered earlier but the total meetings can be discussed now. Administrators must never assume or take for granted that trustees naturally understand the aspects of higher education. They simply do not and must constantly be educated and reeducated concerning all the areas of their supervision. In a great sense the college is the teacher and the board the learner. The only difficulty is that in this case the learners are the "boss." The president must decide before the meeting convenes if the trustees are equipped and prepared with the necessary tools, material, and information necessary for the meeting. He also must decide if his staff that will accompany him to the meeting is equally prepared. Two ill-equipped and ill-prepared groups can make decisions that are disastrous to an institution. If the board is to make an unwise decision, make sure that they had all the information essential to making the wisest one. The president can make a checklist for each meeting and review it before he leaves for that meeting. To convene such a high-powered group and forget materials for the conflab is inexcusable. A good secretary can be the insurance against that embarrassment occuring. Trustees are not looking for excuses but answers.

14. *Have adequate policies been established for guidelines of governorship?*

An institution must determine if there have been devised clear statements of policy to guide the governing board, the president, the administration, and the faculty, as well as the students. The governing board needs unequivocal statements as to its mission and its responsibilities. The president must have his responsibility clearly defined. Once these two areas have been defined, the policy statement regarding administration, faculty, and students can be established. It is true that most guidelines will remain in a constant state of review and adjustment. No board should begin its tenure without the boundary maintenance understood in cogent and effective terms. Many trouble areas could have been avoided if policy statements had been created and then lucidly communicated to the institution. Participation and representation by the affected parties have been clearly involved in its ratification. This means involved from its conception to its birth. The design of these policies can be evaluated only in relationship to their goals—the philosophy of the university. The philosophy of the university and its goals are the primary and most important considerations in policy creation. Its interpretation must be carefully reviewed because it affects its reception immeasurably. Properly structured policies are assets. Whether the precepts of policies are valid and consequential for the growth of the institution will be strikingly apparent and many times forcefully obvious.

15. *Has the board selected a chief administrator and his team of administrators that are capable of handling the institution at its stage of progress?*

It takes one staff to move an academic enterprise. It takes the best equipped staff to move the academic enterprise successfully. The board must review periodically whether they have the best staff to meet the needs of their institution at its particular stage in growth. Universities have their own personalities, and the staff must be adjusted to that uniqueness. The representative of the board is essential to the achievement of any progress.

The second most important consideration is to select individuals to head up that enterprise. There is no magical formula in how many years a president should serve; most boards move cautiously and perhaps too cautiously in the analysis of the chief administrator. Times change and so it may be the best choice to change the chief administrator and in turn his team of administrators. A board must analyze and determine whether the chief administrator and his team are "holding back" or assisting the institution to achieve the plateau it should attain. Many a board has learned too late the demands of an educationally changing society. The wrong team can reverse and stagnate the progress of an institution. No president or staff should serve an institution when either is not equal to fulfilling the goals of the institution. Thus it should be with all board members. Perpetuation of weakness is hardly a sign of strength.

16. *Do you have a rotation policy for chairmanship?*

The chairman of the board and the chairman of each committee needs to be rotated at a regularly scheduled period. If not, then power blocs can be created on the board which may prove unsatisfactory in the long run. In addition, part of the development of leadership, understanding, and educational growth is the rotation of committee chairmanships. It is true that the best committee chairman may not always be available but his expertise will be readily available in the board meetings and is therefore never lost. This is also true for committee assignments; rotation should be done periodically so that each member is exposed to the various aspects of other committees. In the final analysis, the rotation will prove beneficial and be the constant and consistent source of upgrading board members. Rotation should take place annually; most trustees serve quite long periods of time on boards, so rotation need not occur less than yearly. Some board members may desire to remain on certain committees, and this is where the chairman can move wisely and judiciously. At least one or two experts must always serve or remain on a committee in which they have the greatest ability and interests. The needs of the institution may readily determine the regularity of rotation and the committee arrangement.

17. *Reward through recognition of the services of trustees.*

Each institution should have a policy on recognizing trustees for their services to an institution. Trustees are never rewarded financially for their involvement, but there are methods of recognition that are most useful. Letters of appreciation sent by the faculty, or the president are means of such recognition. Special citations of services which are framed or handsomely bound can express proper recognition. Dinner parties, convocations, and special events are all means of honoring trustees. The tendency of most institutions is to do very little honoring of trustees—and that is not good. Respect, recognition, and honor are but small tokens of appreciation. They are however, vital to continued cooperation and must not be overlooked. The trustees are volunteers who devote their time generously to an institution. It is only fitting that on special occasions they be paid honor for efforts. Don't wait until a trustee dies before paying him some token of collective tribute. (Of course posthumously honors are also in order, but should not be the *only* honors.) Some institutions honor trustees by naming a building or hall after a trustee. This prerogative can be good and may be a trend that should be adopted more often, especially since so much building is taking place on college campuses across the country. The initiation of such may have to come through a recommendation of the president or faculty, since a board naming a building after a fellow trustee may be questioned. It is certain that few people would be more worthy than a trustee. It has been the common custom to name buildings after the most generous donors or philanthropists. Whether the choice may be a policy for recognition and its immediate adoption, implementation for trustees is sorely needed and long overdue.

SUMMARY

In-service training is a solution to upgrade the professional educational adeptness of governing boards. The in-service training can focus on the role of the trustees, the place of higher learning in our society, the history and goals of the college, and more especially on new trends in education and innovations of consequence. In-service training should avoid a chronically miscroscopic focus on the single departments or the operational details of a single problem such as dining facilities. An in-service education program should raise the sights so that trustees can with enthusiasm support and indeed call for a better way.

Evaluation of trustees is vital. These questions serve as a good checklist for evaluations: (1) How well do your board members understand the goals of your institution? (2) How well equipped is your board to achieve these goals? (3) How well do you think your trustees understand their role as board members? (4) Have the needs of the college been described so that board members can be intelligently selected to meet these needs? (5) Do you have an in-service education program for your board members? (6) What steps have been taken to reduce or eliminate the weaknesses on the board? (7) Who plans the agenda for board meetings? (8) What members of the faculty, administration, and student body meet regularly with the board at its regular meetings? (9) Is there a proper balance of professional backrounds represented on the board? (10) Is the board of trustees doing the job that it is incorporated to do? (11) Do you want an active, involved board? (12) How available are the trustees? (13) How equipped and prepared for the meetings are the trustees and the appropriate staff? (14) Have adequate policies been established for guidelines of governorship? (15) Has the board selected a chief administrator and his team of administrators capable of handling the institution at its stage of progress? (16) Do you have a rotation for chairmanships? (17) Are the rewards through recognition of the services of trustees adequate?

QUESTIONS

1. What role should the president and the chairman of the governing board assume in the in-service training program?
2. Who is included in the in-service education program?
3. Who is responsible for the overall supervision of the in-service education program for board members?
4. What are the contents of an in-service education program? Outline the activities that should be included.
5. Should the in-service training program change yearly?
6. What type of resources can be used in the in-service education program?
7. What factors contribute to the success of the in-service education program?
8. What factors hinder the success of the in-service education program?
9. How is an in-service education program evaluated?
10. Should there be a budget for in-service education of your board?
11. How can board members be evaluated individually?
12. How can board members be evaluated collectively?

BIBLIOGRAPHY

Ashmore, Frank L. "Trustees are Grown, Not Born," *Pride*, December 1960, pp. 20–24.

Beery, John R., and Mark Murfin. "Meeting Barriers to In-Service Education," *Educational Leadership*, Vol. 17 (March 1960), pp. 351–355.

Coolidge, Charles A. "Training for Trustees," *Association of American Colleges Bulletin*, XLII (December 1956), pp. 510–513.

Corey, Stephen. "Introduction," in National Society for the Study of Education, *In-Service Education*. Chicago: U. of Chicago Press, 1957, Chap. 12, pp. 1–101.

Cummings, E. C. "Some Observations on the Trustees," *School and Society*, LXXVII (January 3, 1953), pp. 1–3.

Davis, Paul H. "Test for Trustees," *College and University Journal*, Vol. 1, No. 1 (Winter 1962), pp. 22–26.

Garrett, Cyril D. "A Study of the In-Service Improvement Programs of Eight Liberal Arts Colleges," Doctoral Dissertation, Unpublished, Michigan State University, East Lansing, 1957.

GEIER, WOODROW A. (ed.). *Effective Trustees, A Report*, National Conference of Trustees for Church Colleges at Lake Junalist, North Carolina, June 26–28, 1959. Nashville, Tennessee: Division of Educational Institutions, Board of Education, The Methodist Church, 1959.

GILCHRIST, ROBERT S., et al. "Organization of Programs of In-Service Education," in National Society for the Study of Education, *In-Service Education*, Chicago: U. of Chicago Press, 1957, Chap. 12, pp. 285–310.

GROSS, RICHARD E. "A Etudy of In-service Education Programs for Student Personnel Workers in Selected Colleges and Universities in the United States," unpublished doctoral dissertation, Michigan State University, East Lansing, 1963.

GUZZETA, DOMONICO. "Growth Through In-Service Training," *Phi Delta Kappan*, Vol. 36 (May 1955), pp. 311–321.

HASS, C. GLENN. "In-Service Education Today," in National Society for the Study of Education, *In-Service Education*. Chicago: U. of Chicago Press, 1957, Chap. 2, pp. 13–34.

HENRY, NELSON. In-Service Education, The Fifty-Sixth Yearbook of the National Society for the Study of Education. Chicago: U. of Chicago Press, 1957.

KELLEY, WILLIAM F. "Twenty Studies of In-Service Education of College Faculty and the Procedures Most Recommended," *Educational Administration and Supervision*, Vol. 36 (October 1956), pp. 351–358.

KINNICH, J. B., et al. "The Teachers and the In-Service Education Program," in National Society for the Study of Education, *In-Service Education*, Chicago: U. of Chicago Press, 1957, Chap. 6, pp. 131–152.

LEWIS, ARTHUR J., et al. "The Role of the Administrator of In-Service Education" in National Society for the Study of Education, *In-Service Education*, Chicago: U. of Chicago Press, 1957, Chap. 7, pp. 153–173.

MERRY, R. W. "How to Orient and Train Trustees," *Liberal Education*, Vol. XLV (October 1959), pp. 373–381.

MISNER, PAUL J. "In-Service Education Comes of Age," Journal of Teacher Education, Vol. 1 (March 1950), pp. 32–36.

National Society for the Study of Education, *In-Service Education*. Chicago: U. of Chicago Press, 1959.

NORRIS, ROBERT B. "Administering In-Service Education in the College," *School and Society*, Vol. 77 (May 1953), pp. 327–329.

PARKER, CECIL J. "Guidelines for In-Service Education," in National Society for the Study of Education, *In-Service Education*. Chicago: U. of Chicago Press, 1957, Chap. 5, pp. 103–128.

RUSSELL, JOHN DALE, and FLOYD W. REEVES. *The Evaluation of Higher Institutions*. Vol. 6: Administration. Chicago: U. of Chicago Press, 1936.

TRUITT, JOHN W. "In-Service Training Programs for Student Personnel Workers," paper presented at the American College Personnel Association annual meeting, Denver, Colorado, April 1961 (mimeo).

WILSON, FRANCIS M. "What Makes An Effective In-Service Training Program?" *Journal of the National Association of Deans of Women*, Vol. 16 (1953), pp. 51–56.

APPENDIX

Bylaws

BYLAWS OF THE BOARD OF TRUSTEES
STATE UNIVERSITY OF NEW YORK

Article I

BOARD OF TRUSTEES

1. *Powers.* The Board of Trustees shall govern the University and shall exercise all of its corporate powers.

2. *Composition: Term: Vacancies.* The Board shall consist of fifteen members appointed by the Governor of the State of New York by and with the advice and consent of the Senate of the State of New York, one of whom shall be designated by the Governor upon appointment as Chairman and one as Vice-Chairman. Vacancies in the membership of the Board shall be filled for the unexpired term in the same manner as original appointments.

3. *Quorum.* At all meetings of the Board eight members shall be necessary and sufficient to constitute a quorum for the transaction of business, and the act of a majority of the members present at any meeting at which a quorum is present shall be the act of the Board, except as otherwise specifically required by law or by these Bylaws; provided, that a majority of the members present at any meeting, although less than a quorum, may adjourn the meeting from time to time without notice other than announcement at the meeting.

4. *Meetings: Notice.* Regular meetings of the Board shall be held at such time and place as shall be determined by the Board. Special meetings may be called at any time by the Chairman, the Vice-Chairman or by any eight members by petition, and shall be held at such time and place as may be fixed in the call of such meeting. At least ten days' notice of every meeting shall be mailed by the Secretary of the Board to the usual address of each Trustee, unless such notice be waived by a majority of the Board.

5. *Chairman and Vice-Chairman.* The Chairman shall exercise the usual functions of a presiding officer and shall have such other powers and duties as may be conferred upon him by the Board. He shall be ex officio a member of all standing and special committees of the Board. In the absence or disability of the Chairman, the Vice-Chairman shall perform the duties and exercise the powers of the Chairman.

6. *Secretary.* During the pleasure of the Board, the Secretary of the Corporation shall be the Secretary of the Board. The Secretary shall keep a record of the proceedings of the Board and shall send copies thereof to each member of the Board. He shall furnish, unless otherwise

159

ordered by the Board, to each of the Trustees a *bound set of minutes*, reports and printed communications of the Board. He shall maintain a complete file of proceedings and reports of all committees of the Board.

Article II
EXECUTIVE COMMITTEE

1. *Composition: Term: Vacancies.* There may be, whenever the Board of Trustees shall by the vote of a majority of the total membership of the Board so determine, an Executive Committee composed of six members of the Board of Trustees, who shall be elected by the Board.

The members elected by the Board shall be chosen at its last regular meeting in each fiscal year on nomination of the Chairman or from the floor. Such elected members shall hold office for one-year terms to commence the April first following such meeting, and until their successors are elected and shall qualify. Vacancies in the unexpired terms of such elected members shall be filled by the Board.

Four members of the Committee shall constitute a quorum.

2. *Secretary.* Unless otherwise specified by the Board or Executive Committee, the Secretary of the Corporation shall be the Secretary of the Executive Committee. It shall be the duty of the Secretary to keep a record of the proceedings of the Executive Committee and to have a copy thereof sent to each member of the Board.

3. *Meetings.* The Executive Committee shall determine the dates and places of its regular meetings and the notice, if any, thereof. Special meetings may be called by its chairman, the Chairman of the Board, or by any three members thereof. Not less than *three days' notice* of special meetings shall be given the members, except that any notice may be waived by all the members either before or after the meeting.

4. *Powers.*
   (a) The Executive Committee may, between meetings of the Board, transact such business of State University as the Board of Trustees may authorize subject to the following limitations:
      (i) It shall not take any action inconsistent with the established policies of the Board or actions which affect the fixed duties of other standing committees of the Board; and
      (ii) It shall not take any actions for which a specified number of votes or a vote by ballot by the Board is required by statute or these Bylaws.
   (b) The Executive Committee shall be charged with the duty of

preparing the budget as required by Chapter 695 of the Laws of 1948 of New York and presenting it to the Board for action.

Article III

COMMITTEES

The Board of Trustees may establish and constitute such standing and special committees as it may from time to time deem desirable, to function until discharged by the Board.

Article IV

OFFICERS

The Board shall appoint its own officers and staff, prescribe the duties of such employees, and fix their compensation within the appropriations prescribed therefore, but in order to coordinate planning functions of the Board with those of the State Education Department at least one of the executive officers shall be a designee of the Commissioner of Education.

Article V

OFFICES

1. *Principal Office.* The principal office of the University shall be located in Albany, New York.

2. *Other Offices.* The University may also have such other offices within the State of New York as may from time to time be designated by the Board of Trustees.

Article VI

SEAL

The corporate seal of the University shall be in such form as shall be adopted by the Board of Trustees.

Article VII

FISCAL YEAR

The fiscal year of the University shall be April 1 to March 31, inclusive.

Article VIII

BALLOTS

Whenever in these Bylaws a vote by ballot is prescribed, said ballots will not be by any single vote cast by one person but by the ballots of all qualified voters who are present and voting, and voting shall be in such manner that it shall not be known for what candidate or candidates any particular voter casts his ballot.

Article IX

AMENDMENTS

These Bylaws may be amended at any meeting of the Board of Trustees, but only by the concurrent vote of a majority of the total membership of the Board, and provided that the members of the Board shall have been notified in advance of the meeting as to the substance of the amendments to be presented.

1) Original Bylaws of the Board of Trustees of State University of New York were adopted by the Temporary Board of Trustees on October 29, 1948, Resolution 48–6.
2) The Bylaws, as set forth in the foregoing pages, were adopted by the permanent Board of Trustees on July 14, 1955—Resolution 55–62 —and supersede the 1948 Bylaws.
3) The Bylaws were amended on April 18, 1963—Resolution 63–75— and such amendments have been included in the foregoing.

BYLAWS OF THE BOARDS OF TRUSTEES OF STATE COLLEGES AS AMENDED TO OCTOBER 4, 1967

Article I

OFFICERS OF THE BOARD

The officers of the Board shall consist of the Chairman, a Vice-Chairman, a Secretary, a Treasurer, an Assistant Treasurer and such other officers as may from time to time be elected by the Board. The Chairman, a Vice-Chairman and a Secretary shall be elected from among the members on September first, at the discretion of the Board. Each of such officers shall hold office until September first of the following year unless his membership on the Board shall terminate before that date—in which case, upon the date of such termination. Each member serving as an officer shall hold office until his successor be elected and shall have qualified. The office of Vice-Chairman and Secretary may be held by the same person. The office of Treasurer shall be held by the Treasurer of the University of Rhode Island. The office of Assistant Treasurer shall be held by the Treasurer of Rhode Island College. The Treasurer and Assistant Treasurer shall not be members of the Board. An Assistant Secretary, who shall perform the duties of the Secretary when the Secretary is absent, may be elected or appointed by the Board. The Assistant Secretary need not be a member of the Board, and if not a member of the Board, shall be paid for his or her services such compensation as may be approved by the Board.

Article II

CHAIRMAN

Section 1. The Chairman shall preside at all meetings of the Board. All notices of meetings of the Board, both regular and special, shall be issued by the Chairman, or—at his request—by the Secretary or Assistant Secretary.

Section 2. All communications, resolutions, reports, petitions and the like addressed to the Board shall be referred to the Chairman for presentation to the Board.

Article III

VICE-CHAIRMAN

Selection 1. In the absence of the Chairman, the Vice-Chairman shall perform the duties of the Chairman.

Section 2. In the absence of both Chairman and Vice-Chairman, a Chairman pro tempore shall be elected from among members of the Board.

Article IV

SECRETARY

Section 1. The record of all business transacted at each meeting including motions made and of actions taken thereupon shall be kept under the direction and supervision of the Secretary.

Section 2. The Secretary or Assistant Secretary, when requested so to do by the Chairman, shall issue notices for meetings of the Board stating insofar as possible the business to be transacted at such meeting and shall transmit to each member of the Board and to the President of each college under the Board's control no later than five days prior to such meeting a copy of the minutes of the last preceding meeting.

Section 3. The Secretary and/or Assistant Secretary shall forthwith upon receipt by him of same transmit to the Chairman for presentation to the Board all communications, resolutions, reports, petitions and the like addressed to the Board.

Article V

COMMUNICATIONS, RESOLUTIONS, REPORTS, ETC.

Communications, resolutions, reports, petitions and the like shall be considered or acted upon by the Board when the same shall be filed with the Chairman or presented at a meeting of the Board at least seven days prior to the meeting at which it shall be considered and copies thereof must be given or mailed to each member of the Board and the President of the college to which the business appertains at least five days prior to such meeting; provided, however, that this requirement may be waived at any meeting of the Board by a vote of at least five members.

Article VI

REGULAR MEETINGS

Section 1. Regular meetings of the Board shall be held on the first Wednesday of each month; provided, however, that if the first Wednesday in any month shall be a legal holiday, the meeting in that month shall be held on the second Wednesday of the month, and provided further that, in his discretion, the Chairman may cancel one or both of the regular meetings otherwise scheduled for the months of July and August. At least five of these regular meetings shall be held at the University of Rhode Island and at least five of them shall be held at Rhode Island College. Notices of the regular meetings, indicating time and place of meeting shall be sent by the Secretary or Assistant Secretary at least five days prior to the day of the meeting.

Section 2. Meetings To Be Open. Meetings of the Board shall be open and accessible to the public, subject to limitations of space and to such reasonable restrictions as shall be imposed by the Chairman or by vote of the Board in particular situations to assure the orderly conduct of business; provided, however, that disciplinary, personnel and confidential matters, the disclosure or public discussion of which would, in the opinion of a majority of the members present, be unduly detrimental to the individuals involved or to the effective discharge of the Board's responsibilities, may be discussed in executive session.

Section 3. Minutes of Meetings. Minutes of open meetings shall be deemed public records. Minutes of executive sessions shall be confidential, but final action taken in executive session shall be reported by the Chairman at the next open meeting of the Board and shall be recorded as part of the minutes of such open meeting.

Section 4. Press and Public Relations. The Chancellor and the Chairman are authorized to release the agenda of open meetings to news media prior to the meeting on condition that no material included therein, other than the identity of the topics to be considered at the meeting, shall be published or broadcast prior to the meeting. The Chairman shall be the chief spokesman for the Board; and the members shall, to the extent possible and consistent with the proper discharge of their individual responsibilities, refer all inquiries which concern interpretation of Board action and policy to the Chairman. The Chancellor is authorized to answer all inquiries concerning the office of the Chancellor and any questions of fact concerning the Board or its actions on other than confidential matters.

Article VII
SPECIAL MEETINGS
Special meetings may be called by the Chairman on his initiative or at the request of any three members of the Board and may be held at any time and place in the State of Rhode Island. Notice of any such meeting shall be sent by certified mail to each member at least five days in advance of the meeting and shall specify the time and place thereof and the object and general character of the business to be transacted thereat; provided, however, that such written notice of a special meeting may be waived by unanimous consent of all nine members of the Board.

Article VIII
QUORUM AND MAJORITY
The presence of any five members of the Board at any duly called regular or special meeting shall constitute a quorum for the transaction

of business. A majority of the members of the Board present at any such meeting, a quorum being present, shall be required for all actions of the Board, and any act of such majority shall be the act of the Board, provided that any such meeting may be adjourned from time to time and from place to place by a majority of the members present, whether or not a quorum is present.

Article IX

Order of Business

At all regular meeting and at special meetings, so far as it may be applicable, the following order of business shall be observed, unless suspended or modified by the Board:

1. Call of meeting to order and establishment of quorum.
2. Consideration of the agenda of the College or the University. The business of the College will be considered first when the Board meets at the University, and the business of the University will be considered first when the Board meets at the College.
3. A combined session shall be held after consideration of the first agenda. During the combined session, the Board shall consider approval of the minutes of the previous meeting and any matters that are of interest or concern to both the University and the College.
4. Consideration of the second agenda.
5. An executive session of the Board may be called by the Chairman for consideration of special matters, including the election of officers.
6. Motion for adjournment.

Article X

Committees

The Board shall create no standing committees or subcommittees. Its policy shall be to consider all matters requiring its attention as a whole without delegating its responsibilities. From time to time the Board may create special advisory committees to make specific investigations and reports and to discharge such other temporary duties as the Board may assign to them, subject always to review and approval or disapproval by the whole Board.

Article XI

Appointees

Section 1. Presidents. The president of each college shall be appointed by the Board for an indefinite term of office at the pleasure of the Board unless such term shall be specifically fixed at the time of his appointment. If and when an appointment is made for a specific term of years, it shall be reviewed not less than one year before its expiration and be extended for the full term or notice by given that it is not to be renewed upon its expiration. If and when an appointment is made for an indefinite term, thereafter the salary of the president will be reviewed annually. He shall administer the affairs of such college subject to the supervision of the Board, and all other officers, instructors and employees of such college shall be responsible to him. He shall be notified of regular and special meetings in the same manner as the members of the Board, and shall have the privilege of attending all sessions except when requested by the Board to withdraw therefrom. He shall have authority to sign all purchase requisitions and vouchers for such college. He shall make such recommendations to the Board from time to time as may seem wise to him, touching any phase of college policy or administration, including without limitation recommendations for appointments to both faculty and administrative staff positions under the Board of Trustees. All communications from any instructor, officer or other employee of either college addressed to the Board shall be transmitted through the president of such college. All replies to such communications and all rules, regulations, directions, orders or any instructions of the Board, addressed to any instructor, officer or other employee of either college shall be transmitted through the president of such college. The president of each college shall perform such other duties as may be provided for by the regulations for such college adopted by the Board.

Section 2. Officers of Administration and Instruction. The Board may at any time appoint, upon the recommendation of the president, such administrative officers and members of the faculty for either college as it may deem necessary for the proper management of such college. The duties of such administrative officers and members of the faculty shall be such as may be provided for by regulations for such college adopted by the Board.

Article XII

SALARIES OF ADMINISTRATIVE OFFICERS
AND MEMBERS OF THE FACULTY

The salary of every administrative officer and member of the faculty appointed by the Board upon recommendation of the president shall be fixed by the Board at or before the time of his appointment.

Article XIII

FISCAL YEAR AND FISCAL ROUTINE

Section 1. The fiscal year of the Board, for which its budget shall be made and upon which its other fiscal summaries and reports shall be based, shall be the same as the fiscal year fixed by law for the general financial affairs of the State of Rhode Island.

Section 2. The president of each institution shall present a proposed budget to the Board for its consideration. Upon Board approval of the proposed annual budgets for the colleges, said budgets shall be transmitted by the Board, with the assistance of the president of each college, to the Budget Officer of the State of Rhode Island at such time as will permit its consideration and transmitted to the General Assembly prior to the date when the annual appropriation for the colleges shall be made. After the General Assembly has approved the budget and/or authorized an appropriation for each college, the Board shall direct each president to prepare and submit to the Board the operating budget. Upon approval by the Board, the operating budget becomes the budget authority for the expenditures under the direction of the president.

Section 3. At the end of each quarter of the fiscal year, the president of each college shall present to the Board a statement of the expenditures for the previous quarter for such college. This statement shall also show the unexpired balance in each account.

Section 4. Every purchase requisition for either college shall be approved either by the comptroller or business manager or his delegated representative. Properly approved copies of such requisitions shall be sent directly to the State Purchasing Agent.

Section 5. All vouchers for expenditures by either college shall be approved by an appropriate official of such college, and this approval shall be sufficient to authorize the State Comptroller to honor such vouchers.

Section 6. Each annual budget and quarterly statement pertaining to the Rhode Island College shall be separated between the College and the Henry Barnard School, and each such budget and statement pertaining to the University of Rhode Island shall be separated among the College, the Experiment Station and the Extension Service.

Article XIV

AMENDMENTS

These bylaws may be amended, extended or repealed in whole or in part at any meeting of the Board by simple majority vote of the members present, provided that the text of any proposed amendment, addition, or repealer shall have been mailed by the Secretary or Assistant Secretary to each member of the Board and to the President of each college under its control at least one week in advance of the date of such meeting.

Article XV

REPEAL OF INCONSISTENT ACTS

Insofar as any other bylaws and acts of the Board are inconsistent herewith, the same are hereby repealed.

*(Article **XVI**. Amended to establish policy for open meetings.)*

(When the term "Board" shall be used in this document, it shall mean the Board of Trustees of State Colleges. When the term "colleges" shall be used in this document, it shall mean that one of the colleges therein referred to shall be understood to refer to the University of Rhode Island.)

BYLAWS OF WESTMONT COLLEGE

Article I

CORPORATE SEAL

The Corporation shall have a corporate seal consisting of a circle having on its circumference the words "WESTMONT COLLEGE, Christus Primatum Tenens," and in the center thereof the word "INCORPORATED" followed by the date May 22, 1940 and the word "CALIFORNIA."

Article II

OFFICES

Section 1. Principal Office. The Principal office for the transaction of the business of the corporation shall, until changed by the trustees, be at the office of the Secretary, Fourth Floor, 611 Shatto Place, in the City and County of Los Angeles, State of California. The Board of trustees is hereby granted full power and authority to change said principal office from one location to another in said county.

Section 2. Other Offices. Branch of subordinate offices may at any time by established by the board of trustees at any place or places where the corporation is qualified to do business.

Article III

MEETING OF MEMBERS

Section 1. Place of Meetings The annual meetings of members and all other meetings of members shall be held either at the principal office or any other place within or without the State of California which may be designated either by the board of trustees, pursuant to authority hereinafter granted to said board, or by the written consent of all members entitled to vote thereat, given either before or after the meeting and filed with the Secretary of the corporation.

Section 2. Annual Meetings. The annual meetings of the members shall be held on the fourth Friday of October of each year at 1:30 o'clock P.M. of said day; provided, however, that should said day fall upon a legal holiday, then any such annual meeting of members shall be held at the same time and place on the next day thereafter ensuing which is not a legal holiday.

Written notice of each annual meeting shall be given to each member entitled to vote by sending a copy of the notice through the mail or telegraph, charges prepaid, to his or her last known address appearing on the books of the corporation or supplied by him or her to the corporation for the purpose of notice. If a member supplies no address, notice shall be deemed to have been given to him or her if mailed to the place where the principal office of the corporation is situated, or in the alternative, published at least once in some newspaper of general circulation in the County of said principal office. All such notices shall be sent to each member entitled thereto not less than five days before each annual meeting, and shall specify the place, the day, and the hour of such meeting.

Section 3. Special Meetings. Special meetings of members for any purpose or purposes whatsoever may be called at any time by the President of the board of trustees, or by any two members thereof.

Notice of such special meetings shall be given in the same manner as for annual meetings of members. Notices of any special meeting shall specify, in addition to the place, day and hour of such meeting, the general nature of the business to be transacted.

Section 4. Adjourned Meetings and Notice Thereof. Any meetings of the members, annual or special, whether or not a quorum is present, may be adjourned from time to time by the vote of a majority of the members who are either present in person or represented by proxy thereat, but in the absence of a quorum no other business may be transacted at any such meeting.

Section 5. Voting at All Meetings of Members. Every member entitled to vote shall have the right to vote in person or by proxy. Said proxy, however, must be given to some other person who is a member.

Section 6. Quorum. The presence in person or by proxy of a majority of the members entitled to vote at any meeting shall constitute a quorum for the transaction of business. The members present at a duly called or held meeting at which a quorum is present may continue to do business until adjournment, notwithstanding the withdrawal of enough members to leave less than a quorum.

Section 7. Consent of Absentees. The transactions of any meeting of members, either annual or special, however called and noticed, shall be as valid as though had at a meeting duly held after regular call and notice, if a quorum be present either in person or by proxy, and if either before or after the meeting each of the members entitled to vote not present in person or by proxy sign a written waiver of notice or a consent to the holding of such meeting, or an approval of the minutes thereof. All such waivers, consents or approvals shall be filed with the corporate records or made a part of the minutes of the meeting.

Section 8. Proxies. Every person entitled to vote or execute consents, shall have the right to do so either in person or by an agent authorized by a written proxy executed by such person in favor of some other member and filed with the Secretary of the corporation; provided that no such proxy shall be valid after the expiration of eleven months from the date of execution.

Article IV

TRUSTEES

Section 1. Powers. Subject to limitations of the Articles of incorporation and of the Bylaws, and subject to the duties of trustees as prescribed by the Bylaws, all corporate powers shall be exercised by or under the authority of, and the business and affairs of the corporation shall be controlled by a board of trustees without prejudice to such general powers, but subject to the same limitations, it is hereby expressly declared that the trustees shall have the following powers, to wit:

First: To elect by ballot, annually, one of their number as President of the board.

Second: Upon the death, or other vacancy in the office, or expiration of the term of any trustee, to elect another in his place who shall hold office for the same time and under the conditions described in the Bylaws of the corporation, provided, that where there are graduates prescribe, nominate persons to fill vacancies in the board of trustees. Such nominations shall be considered by the board, but it may reject any and all such nominations, and of its own motion appoint others.

Third: To elect additional trustees, provided the whole number elected shall never exceed thirty at one time.

Fourth: To declare vacant the seat of any Trustees who shall absent themselves from four successive meetings of the Board except for a long illness or absence from this country.

Fifth: To receive and hold by purchase, gift, devise, bequest or grant, real or personal property for educational purposes connected with the corporation, or for the benefit of the institution.

Sixth: To sell, mortgage, lease and otherwise use and dispose of the property of the corporation in such manner as they shall deem most conducive to the prosperity of the corporation.

Seventh: To direct and prescribe the course of study and discipline to be observed in the college or seminary.

Eighth: To appoint a president of the college or seminary who shall hold his office during the pleasure of the trustees.

Ninth: To appoint such professors, tutors, and other officers as they shall deem necessary, who shall hold their offices during the pleasure of the trustees.

Tenth: To grant such honors as are usually granted by any university, college or seminary of learning in the United States, and in testimony thereof to give suitable diplomas under their seal, and the signature of such officers of the corporation and the institution as they shall deem expedient.

Eleventh: To fix salaries of the president, professors, and other officers and employees of the college or seminary.

Twelfth: To make all bylaws and ordinances necessary and proper to carry into effect the preceding powers and necessary to advance the interests of the college or seminary, provided that no bylaws or ordinances shall conflict with the Constitution or laws of the United States, or of this State.

Section 2. Number and Qualification of Trustees. The board of trustees shall consist of the number of trustees named in the Articles of Incorporation until changed by amendment thereto.

Section 3. Election and Term of Office. The trustees to be elected each year shall be elected at each annual meeting of the members, but if any such annual meeting is not held, or the trustees are not elected thereat, the trustees may be elected at any special meeting of members held for that purpose. All trustees shall hold office until their respective successors are elected, and for the terms set out in the Articles of Incorporation and any amendment thereto except that for the first year three trustees shall be elected for three years, three trustees for two years, and three trustees for one year, respectively.

Section 4. Vacancies. Vacancies in the board of trustees may be filled by a majority of the remaining trustees and each trustee so elected shall hold office until his successor is elected at an annual meeting of the members or at a special meeting called for that purpose. A vacancy or vacancies shall be deemed to exist in case of death, removal out of state, resignation, removal or refusal of any trustee to qualify in the manner provided in Article Seven of the Articles of Incorporation.

Section 5. Place of Meeting. All meetings of the board of trustees shall be held at the principal office of the corporation, or at any other place within or without the State of California, designated at any time by resolution of the board or by written consent of all members of the board.

Section 6. Organization Meeting. Immediately following each annual meeting of the members, the board of trustees shall hold a regular meeting for the purpose of organization, election of officers, and the transaction of other business. Notice of such meetings is hereby dispensed with.

Section 7. Other Regular Meetings. Other regular meetings of the board of trustees shall be held without call, on the fourth Friday of the following months: January, April, July and October, at 1:30 o'clock P.M.

of said day, provided, however, that should said day fall upon a legal holiday then said meeting shall be held at the same time on a convenient day thereafter ensuing which is not a legal holiday. Notice of such meetings of the board of trustees is hereby dispensed with.

Section 8. Special Meetings. Special meetings of the board of trustees for any purpose or purposes shall be called at any time by the President; if he or she is absent or unable or refuses to act, by the Vice President, or upon the request of at least two trustees.

Written notice of the time and place of special meetings shall be delivered personally to the trustees or sent to each trustee by letter or by telegram, charges prepaid, addressed to him or her at his or her address as it is shown upon the records of the corporation, or if it is not shown on such records or is not readily ascertainable, at the place in which the meetings of the trustees are regularly held. In case such notice is mailed or telegraphed, it shall be deposited in the United States mail or delivered to the telegraph company in the place at which the principal office of the corporation is located, at least forty-eight (48) hours prior to the time of the holding of the meeting. In case such notice is delivered as above provided, it shall be so delivered at least twenty-four (24) hours prior to the time of the holding of the meeting. Such mailing, telegraphing or delivery as above provided shall be due, legal and personal notice to such trustees.

Section 9. Notice of Adjournment. Notice of adjournment of any trustees' meeting, either regular or special, need not be given to absent trustees if the time and place are fixed at the meeting adjourned.

Section 10. Waiver of Notice. The transactions of any meeting of the board of trustees, however called and noticed or wherever held, shall be as valid as though had at a meeting duly held after regular call and notice, if a quorum be present, and if either before or after the meeting each of the trustees not present sign a written waiver of notice or a consent to hold such meeting or an approval of the minutes thereof. All such waivers, consents or approvals shall be filed with the corporate records or made a part of the minutes of the meeting.

Section 11. Quorum. A majority of the members of the board of trustees shall be necessary to constitute a quorum for the transaction of business, except to adjourn, as hereinafter provided. Every act or decision done or made by a majority of the trustees present at a meeting duly held at which a quorum is present shall be regarded as the act of the board of trustees.

Section 12. Adjournment. A quorum of the trustees may adjourn any trustees' meeting to meet again at a stated day and hour; provided, however, that in the absence of a quorum a majority of the trustees present at any trustees' meeting, either regular or special, may adjourn from time to time until the time fixed for the next regular meeting of the board.

Section 13. Assent in Writing. Any action of the members of the board of trustees, although not at a regular or special meeting, if assented to in writing by all of the members of the board, and filed with the Secretary, shall be as valid and effective in all respects as if passed by the board in regular meeting. Whenever all members of the board entitled to vote at any meeting of trustees consent to any measure by writing either on the records of the proceedings or filed with the Secretary, such actions shall be as valid as if had at a meeting regularly called, and any business thus transacted or direction or orders given and made shall be as effective and valid as though had and done at a regular meeting of the board.

Section 14. Executive Committee. An Executive Committee of three or more trustees may be appointed by the board of trustees from their number to serve at the pleasure of said board for the transaction of such business of the corporation as may require their attention between the meetings of the board of trustees of this corporation. All business transacted by such Committee shall be subject to the approval of the board of trustees at their next regular or special meeting.

A majority of the Committee shall constitute a quorum for the transaction of business, and any act or decision done or made by this majority shall be regarded as the act or decision of the Committee. However, nothing contained in this Section shall give the Committee the authority or power to adopt, amend or repeal the Bylaws.

Section 15. Other Committees. The board of trustees may appoint other committees of three or more trustees to serve at the pleasure of the said board for the transaction of other business (except that of the Executive Committee) that may be required of them between the meetings of the board of trustees of this corporation, providing no authority or power of the board of trustees is delegated to them. All business transacted by such committee shall be subject to the approval of the board of trustees at their next regular or special meeting.

A majority of a committee shall constitute a quorum for the transaction of each committee's business, and any act or decision done or made by this majority of each committee shall be regarded as the act or decision of such committee.

However, this section does not in any way apply to or affect Article V of these Bylaws.

Article V

ADVISORY BOARD OF NONMEMBERS

An Advisory Board of nonmembers of this corporation may be appointed by the board of trustees to advise and counsel them on important matters coming before the board. The term of office and the number of members are to be determined by the board of trustees and such nonmembers are to serve at the pleasure of the board of trustees and are not entitled to vote nor are they entitled to exercise any of the rights of membership in this corporation.

Article VI

OFFICERS

Section 1. Officers. The officers of the corporation shall be chairman, a vice-chairman, a secretary and a treasurer, and such other officers as the board of trustees may determine, which officers shall be elected by and hold office, at the pleasure of the board of trustees. The secretary and treasurer may be one and the same person.

Section 2. Compensation and Tenure. The compensation and tenure of all of the officers of the corporation shall be fixed and determined by the board of trustees.

Article VII

QUALIFICATION AND RIGHTS OF MEMBERS

Every member of this corporation and every teacher, professor, assistant professor, lecturer and missionary employed by this corporation shall be persons over twenty-one (21) years of age and shall be required to subscribe to the Articles of Faith set out in the Articles of Incorporation in the month of June in each year, or in the alternative, when the Fall semester begins.

Any member of the corporation ceasing to believe the whole or any part of said Articles of Faith shall, by reason of that fact, be disqualified from being or remaining a member or trustee of this corporation, and shall forthwith cease to be such member or trustee.

No teaching inconsistent with said Articles of Faith shall be tolerated on the part of any teacher, missionary or other agent employed by this corporation, and such teaching shall be cause for immediate dismissal.

Every member of this corporation shall be automatically elected to membership upon their becoming a trustee of this corporation. Said board of trustees shall also have the power to suspend or expel any members of this corporation in accordance with the Articles of Incorporation and these Bylaws.

Article VIII

AMENDMENTS

These Bylaws may be amended or altered at any meeting of the trustees duly assembled by a majority vote of those present, provided notice of the proposed amendment shall have been given or waived at least ten days prior to said meeting.

Article IX

ENDOWMENTS

All property either real or personal or both, given for endowment purposes to this nonprofit religious and educational corporation by deed, will or otherwise, and the proceeds derived therefrom by sale, investment or otherwise (unless the endowment provides to the contrary or is not so restricted), shall forever be held inviolate as a trust fund to promote the purpose of this corporation as declared in its Articles of Incorporation heretofore filed with the Secretary of State of the State of California, and only the net income arising from or derived through said property so given shall ever be expended; but all of said property or the proceeds derived from the sale or sales thereof, shall be forever kept separate from the other property of this corporation as a permanent endowment fund; provided, however, that the net annual income derived from said property so donated to this corporation may be used for the promotion of the said purposes of this corporation in such manner and at such times as may be determined by its board of trustees. Separate books of account shall be kept showing accurately the details of such endowment fund and the property or securities in which the same may be invested.

Article X

TRUSTEES EMERITI

Section 1. Eligibility. There is hereby created the office of Trustee Emeritus, to which there shall be eligible retiring Trustees (either by resignation or expiration of term) who (1) have been Trustees for ten (10) years or longer, and/or (2) are past the age of seventy years, and (3) have not found themselves able to attend stated meetings of the Board.

Section 2. Names—College Catalog and Right to Participate in Deliberation of Board of Trustees. Trustees Emeriti shall have their names as such carried in the college catalogue, and shall be entitled to participate fully in the deliberations of the Board but shall not have the right to vote on any such matters.

[Adopted November 14, 1958]

SECRETARY'S CERTIFICATE OF ADOPTION OF BYLAWS

Certificate of Secretary

I, the undersigned, hereby certify:

(1) That I am the duly elected and acting secretary of WESTMONT COLLEGE, a California nonprofit religious and educational corporation; and

(2) That the foregoing Bylaws comprising eleven (11) pages, including this page, constitute the original Bylaws of said corporation as duly adopted at the first meeting of the board of trustees thereof, duly held July 26th, 1940.

IN WITNESS WHEREOF, I have hereunto subscribed my name and affixed the seal of said corporation this 26th day of July, 1940.

/s/   Mrs. A. H. Kerr
Secretary

[SEAL]

Index